# praise for *anything*

"*Anything* does theology without hanging out a sign. Intersecting everyday issues, Jennie carefully plants God's word inside the heart, in the weak and discolored places, so we can be strengthened by grace and flower in truth. This is a success in its own right, but Jennie does more. She writes not as a detached observer but as a friend, inviting you to sit down for coffee and open up your heart while she pours in grace. Pull up a chair, crack the book, and open your heart. You'll be glad you did."

JONATHAN DODSON
Author, *Gospel-Centered Discipleship*
Pastor, Austin City Life

"Jennie Allen is a visionary, a girlfriend, and a Jesus-chaser. I can't think of three qualities I more appreciate in a woman. I loved this book from cover to cover and have been really contemplating the way a one-word prayer can affect one's heart and ministry in this life. I want to be an 'anything' kind of girl, and I appreciate and respect the example Jennie has set in pursuing God and what he desires in us. It's just a word on paper, but it's a lifetime choice that can make all the difference. You in?"

ANGIE SMITH
Speaker, Women of Faith
Author, *I Will Carry You* and *What Women Fear*

"If you are content, comfortable, and satisfied with life as you know it now, don't read this book. By writing *Anything*, Jennie has become to me what she calls a 'spiritual domino.' I have been affected deeply by her passion and, more important, by the Lord's voice through her to the point that I couldn't help but fall on my face and cry to him, 'Anything!'"

LAUREN CHANDLER
Speaker, Singer, Wife of Matt Chandler—The Village Church

"Jennie Allen is one of those people you remember long after you meet her. When it comes to communicating God's truths, she is passionate, relevant, and authentic to the core. I'm excited to see where God leads her and will be cheering her on all the way!"

VICKI COURTNEY
Speaker and Author, *Five Conversations*

"In her book *Anything*, Jennie Allen issues an invitation to simply pray, *God, I will do anything.* She doesn't presume to know what that will mean for me, which is perhaps one of the main reasons why I trust her voice as a communicator. Jennie doesn't push me to a certain radical act or a dramatic experience. With a fresh perspective on surrender, she simply points believers to Jesus and challenges us to actually *believe.* I can't stop talking about this powerful book."

EMILY P. FREEMAN
Author, *Grace for the Good Girl*

"It's this simple: if every believer prayed this prayer, lived his or her own story with this type of abandon, the gospel would be unleashed in every corner on earth, including the darkest corners of our own hearts. Jennie has given us a true gift. Read, receive, discuss, then run straight into your own 'anything.'"

JEN HATMAKER
Author, *Interrupted* and *Seven*

"Jennie Allen's *Anything* is the kind of book you *have* to put down. Expect your reading to be interrupted by the overwhelming desire to get on your knees and beg God to help you utter the impossible word: anything. Between each chapter I discovered new scraps of my heart to surrender to him, and with the turn of every page I felt fresh joy bubbling up in me at the possibility of living a life where God gets everything. Reading this book wasn't an intellectual exercise. It was a transforming experience."

FABIENNE HARFORD
Women's Discipleship
Austin Stone Community Church

"Jennie Allen tells her story with transparency, honesty, and humor. She is one of those rare writers who does not take herself too seriously but takes God very seriously! She includes the reader on her spiritual quest to see where her 'anything' prayer will take her. This book will encourage anyone of any age who is exploring what it means to surrender everything to God."

SUSIE HAWKINS
Bible Study Teacher
Author, *From One Ministry Wife to Another*

"In her book *Anything*, Jennie Allen gives me great hope for the church in our American culture. At a time when droves of younger adults are leaving the church, Jennie and her husband Zac have discovered what authentic faith is all about. To me, Jennie represents a growing movement of individuals like Francis Chan, David Platt, and others, who deeply desire to follow Jesus in every way. Jesus taught us that following him was not easy. In *Anything*, Jennie is honest and open about her journey, from the struggles of letting go to the peace that only Jesus can provide. Jennie is transparent, honest, rooted in Scripture, and a gifted communicator."

STEVE CARR
Executive Director, Flannel

"My heart is deeply stirred after reading *Anything*. I stand beside Jennie Allen in this fresh movement of unbridled surrender to God . . . grateful for the lives *Anything* will forever change. A compelling, powerful read!"

LISA WHITTLE
Speaker, Advocate, Author, *{w}hole* and *Behind Those Eyes*

"Jennie Allen is a fresh, energetic voice in today's world with great insight into what modern women both want and need."

ROBERT LEWIS
Author, *Men's Fraternity*

"Whether we're crying on bathroom floors or sitting behind cubicle desks, there is a small voice within demanding more. Not the hollow American version of more, but the belief there is more than the bare line of existence. Because there is. More.

"When the belief of *more* meets the desire to do *anything*, the fearful becomes fearless, the wanderer becomes the leader, and the doubter becomes the believer. Because when we pray audacious prayers promising God to do anything, he shows up.

"In Jennie Allen's book *Anything*, the pages unfold and undo the knotted chain of purpose, desire, and the quest to do more by agreeing to do *anything*. If there was a book to open the door to reckless abandon and complete surrender, it's *Anything*. I'm waiting for the floodgates to flail open with women pouring out, shouting fiercely that they are willing and ready to do anything. And I'll be one of them!"

BIANCA JUAREZ OLTHOFF
Teacher, Speaker, Chief Storyteller for the A21 Campaign

"It's been a great joy to know Jennie for most of my life. She radiates sincerity, wisdom, and godly leadership. I'm excited for you to get to know her too."

JOHN SOWERS
Author, *Fatherless Generation*

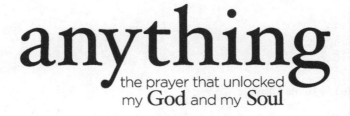

# anything

the prayer that unlocked
my **God** and my **Soul**

## jennie allen

THOMAS NELSON
*Since 1798*

NASHVILLE  DALLAS  MEXICO CITY  RIO DE JANEIRO

Published in Nashville, Tennessee, by Thomas Nelson. Thomas Nelson is a registered trademark of Thomas Nelson, Inc.

Thomas Nelson, Inc., titles may be purchased in bulk for educational, business, fund-raising, or sales promotional use. For information, please e-mail SpecialMarkets@ThomasNelson.com.

Unless otherwise noted, Scripture quotations are taken from THE ENGLISH STANDARD VERSION. © 2001 by Crossway Bibles, a division of Good News Publishers.

**Library of Congress Cataloging-in-Publication Data**

Allen, Jennie.
  Anything : the prayer that unlocked my God and my soul / Jennie Allen.
    p. cm.
  ISBN 978-0-8499-4705-6 (trade paper)
  1. Christian life. 2. Prayer—Christianity. I. Title.
  BV4501.3.A457 2012
  242—dc23                                                    2011053185

*Printed in the United States of America*

12 13 14 15 16 QG 5 4 3 2 1

zac,

you make me love Jesus more.

thank you.

# contents

# my anything

"God we will do anything. *Anything.*"

Zac and I climbed into bed on a completely average night two years ago. We were pretty tired. We just laid there looking at the ceiling, with only small firework fantasies of what God might say. Zac took my hand and spoke the simple words we had been processing for the past few months but not yet been ready to say.

God had been opening our eyes to how precious our temporary lives were and how numbly we were moving through them.

We were over it. We were over building our lives. We were over houses and cars and cute Christmas cards. We wanted something; we couldn't put our finger on it. It was burning in us. We had loved so many other things more than God.

We were ready to do anything.

So we prayed. As sincerely as I have ever prayed any other thing, I prayed in my heart as Zac spoke:

"God we will do anything. *Anything.*"

It didn't feel fancy. It wasn't even a big deal. But the prayer held in it a thousand little deaths. In saying *anything*, it meant we were handing him everything.

My heart raced a little at the thought . . . and then we fell asleep.

## PART 1

::

everything
keeping us from
anything

# plastic god
## abandoning unbelief

"Get off the phone and come in here, Jennie!" I was sixteen.

I got off the phone with my boyfriend and headed into the kitchen. My two little sisters were already sitting at our kitchen table. Everything felt good. Mom always went all out at Christmas—food and decorations, like something out of a magazine but better because you could smell and feel it. Christmas felt important and set apart.

The table had a wreath in the middle with candles sprinkled through it. I knew what we were doing. We did it most Sunday nights each December. We sat and sang—yes, our family of five awkwardly sang hymns around our table. We talked about Christmas and what happened on that night thousands of years ago. It's called *advent*, a beautiful tradition of focusing on Christ throughout the month of Jesus' birth.

We each held a candle while we sang (one year my little sister caught her bangs on fire). Then Dad read a story about the coming Christ and teach us a lesson we could learn from it.

I remember he seemed a little tense that night; it seemed like a lot of work. Looking back, I realize he was doing his best to give us God.

But how do you give someone God?

There were stories on felt boards about Noah's ark and Samson. There were lessons at Sunday school about how I shouldn't gossip or have sex yet. But how do you give someone God?

I never questioned those nights or appreciated them. I was neutral.

Honestly, I felt neutral about God. When you grow up with the stories and songs and lessons, you accept everything; you aren't trying to explain God if you grew up hearing about him since birth, like Santa Claus. I knew what I thought I needed to know. I didn't feel much, for the most part, when watching people talk about him. I don't remember it feeling very real. In fact, I remember God feeling a little plastic.

## How do you give someone God?

He was like a plastic statue on our mantel. In my child's mind, it seemed my family was revolving around the statue; we all would talk to the statue and about the statue. But to me, he was just a statue, a figurehead in our home that felt unmovable. Static. Stale. Unconcerned. Our plastic God. I looked into other families, and as I got older, I even tried my best to look into people's souls. Most of them seemed to have a plastic God too.

Falling in love with God was an intangible concept to me. I knew it was part of the whole deal, the package. I had heard that along the way in some of the lessons. I just didn't know how to truly relate to the plastic statue. Even if I could look past the plastic, then he was just invisible. How do you fall in love with someone invisible?

I wanted to feel something. I wanted it to be real. I needed it to be real. But how do you make something like God real?

You don't. You can't.

4

plastic god

I was the type to play along. I wasn't faking; I just lived in a place that issued scripts. Everyone took theirs and played it. Mine was handed to me, and I played it as sincerely as I could . . . It wasn't fake; it was just my normal.

**Plastic gods are safe. Plastic gods don't mess with you.**

I was a good girl, from a good family and a good church and a good school, who made good grades and had good friends and made good decisions and even had a good dog. I was a good Christian. I mean, I should have been—I had heard the stories, songs, and lessons 7,338 times. It's what I knew.

But God?

I don't remember God, the real God, being there. He probably was. But I just didn't see him—till I did.

You can't control seeing God. That is left to his own discretion—how or when people really see, really get him. But I needed God to not be plastic before I trusted him, especially with everything.

Plastic gods are safe. Plastic gods don't mess with you. Plastic gods don't matter much; they fit in a small crevice of the life you want, the life you were planning to have. And when everything in life is working . . . plastic gods feel like enough.

# red lights

Unbelief is not just something attributed to an atheist or agnostic. Unbelief is found in nooks and spaces within Christianity. Every sin, at its root, is based in something we do not fully believe about God.

Recently, as I was about to actually sign the contract to write this book, I was staring at a stoplight on my way home. I was about to give my life to writing about and talking about my God (or at least the next few years). I was, in essence, taking my faith to such a public level that if he weren't real, it'd be a waste or very fake.

I sat at the stoplight long enough to have a complete crisis of

anything

faith. I pictured heaven and angels and hell and God in heaven and Christ on earth . . . and I thought it all seemed like a tremendous long shot, so far from the reality of my days . . . car pool and laundry and vacations—all the stuff sane people spend time thinking about.

In the questioning it felt as though someone were ripping away every safe and precious thing I held. And then I remembered. I remembered the evidence of his hand even that day in my life, his undeniable presence in my soul as I have suffered or felt him leading me. The marked changes to the insides of me that were not a result of my effort. All of it was screaming of something more—tangible spiritual realities. Green light. Faith crisis was over.

Doubt is in all of us . . . if we go there. If we let it rush in every once in a while.

⁂

Laura's crisis of faith lasted longer than a red light.

Something in her eyes and her voice was incredibly serious, "I don't know what I believe anymore. I am not sure I even believe in Jesus."

Laura went to our church. She was a deep, raw person with whom I eagerly grabbed time whenever kids and schedules allowed. Laura grew up as a pastor's kid in a world that was similar to mine. She went on to work for a college ministry until she had her second son. Laura was the best of the good girls. She knew the rules and she played her part well. God was real because her mom and dad had always told her he was. God had always been such a big part of her life that she never questioned what life would be like without him. She married a good man and had two good children and attended a good church. And yet she was questioning all of it, wondering if any of it had ever been real.

She felt guilty for questioning; she honestly did not even know how to question. Life's realities were causing her to wonder why she'd ever believed in the first place, if her faith had ever been truly hers, or if she just believed because that was all she'd ever known. As we talked, I felt the Lord leading me to encourage her down this road.

"Laura, God can handle your questions, but don't drag this out. Go there and then decide if he is real or not."

She cried, fearing what her family would think, fearing what life would feel like if she did not believe in the God everybody she loved feared. But it was as if God was giving this good little girl permission to wrestle with him. The God of the universe was lovingly saying, "It's okay."

She kept this picture in her mind as she questioned, a picture of a weak and tired soul standing on the top of a tall, far-reaching sky-scraper. God, in the form of a strong, well-grounded crane, swept her up and let her to look over the edge of faith. She peered over into options, visions of things she'd never explored or chosen to see. God graciously led her jump, and yet she felt him holding her out there as she swung for over a year, searching.

Laura would go on to give God everything with me, and he turned her life completely upside down. But his journey for Laura had to begin with Laura deciding whether or not Christ was the way. Until that was secure, everybody was just playing house.

## defining intangibles

Unbelief is no small thing. It lays the foundation for all the places we struggle, and ultimately faith in Christ is what will separate those who belong to God from those who do not.

Usually we do not fear God. We do not see him for who he is; we doubt him. We belittle him. It is the most damaging thing in us—to mistake God for something small or wavering. Yet we leave the doubts alone in us, thinking they are our simple, fickle thoughts.

A. W. Tozer wrote, "What comes into our minds when we think about God is the most important thing about us."[1] Nothing defines a soul more than what that soul believes about God. And no outward observer can know what is in the soul of a person. The most important thing about us is truly only known and defined by the owner of the soul and the one who created it. Everyone else only sees what we want them to see. Nothing defines us more . . . nothing is more important than what we believe about God.

I used to think knowing *about* God was the same as knowing him. I remember sitting in a room full of future pastors at seminary. I always felt out of place. Maybe it was because I was a girl; maybe it was because I sat tearing up listening to professors talk about God while everybody else was taking notes and arguing dispensationalism.

As God was being dissected in front of me, I kept looking around at all those guys, thinking, *Did you hear that?! This is ludicrous.* I was freaking out as we talked about angels and hell and how our souls transform the second we trust Christ. Come on, people. It's insane.

 

At the lake one weekend, I had a deep conversation with a close friend that triggered a big question for me: how does someone know God? She strongly believed the only way someone knows God is through reading Scripture. I agreed. We do not know God apart from Scripture, and every other experience must be held up to his Word, since it is the clearest revelation from him. It was the foundation for every understanding I held about God. I clung to it as I would the very words of God because I believe that is, in fact, what Scripture is. But it still seemed too simple to me. I knew that experiences, friends, prayer life, worship, church, and books had also brought me closer to God . . . helped me to know him.

On Monday I posed the question in class to one of my favorite professors. The answer that followed went on to shape my view of God. He began by listing all the ways we grow or know God: prayer, studying Scripture, church, worship, experiences, suffering, confession, community, and on and on. Then he said, "But obviously each of these is unpredictable . . . many people who study the Bible never find God. Many people who go to church never really know him. The only exercise that works 100 percent of the time to draw one close to the real God is risk."

I think the whole class started questioning him . . . looking for proof text in our minds, trying to find a category for what he had just said.

I started craving . . . a reckless faith, a faith where I knew God was real because I needed him, a faith where I lived surrendered, obedient, a faith where I sacrificed something . . . comfort or safety or practicality . . . something.

Then he went on, "To risk is to willingly place your life in the hand of an unseen God and an unknown future, then to watch him come through. He starts to get real when you live like that."

We were all speechless. Knowing God, really knowing him, was getting more complicated. But if he was real, if he was God, then certainly he was worth knowing—not just the facts, but knowing what it is like to run with him, lean on him, have his hand alone holding us up.

Scripture describes a radical, reoriented life for those who trust Christ—one full of living for the invisible and the future. It is a life fully surrendered to an invisible God whose agenda for my time here is contrary to my own, a life very different from the safe, comfortable one I was creating.

I started craving something that had never seemed acceptable to me until that day . . . a reckless faith, a faith where I knew God was real because I needed him, a faith where I lived surrendered, obedient, a faith where I sacrificed something . . . comfort or safety or practicality . . . something. But my heart raced faster when I thought of it, and something about it resonated.

Stepping out wholly dependent on God to come through, stepping away from what is secure and comfortable exposes the holes in our faith. And then if God comes through, it expands our faith. Something about stepping off cliffs where God leads allows God the opportunity to move in greater ways. When we step off and he shows up, we see him differently than we would if we were standing safely looking over the edge.

## sticky crosses

The first night I saw Jesus I was seventeen. I was sitting, looking up at a lumber cross. I sat in front of the crosses every year at Kanakuk Kamp. I had seen the nailed pieces of wood at least five years running. The campfire was crackling, and three men hung there on a sticky night in July, reenacting the day Christ died, the day his very visible, warm body hung there in a similar way.

But that night I saw him. I saw my sin and how it put him there. I saw the cost. I saw his mercy, and my heart moved. What Christ did on a cross—he bought me; he died so I wouldn't. My plastic god broke, and a new, unsettling God rushed in. I felt him.

We are fleshy, feely creatures. We love things to feel real; we want them to feel warm and tangible and to move through us, and at least make our hearts beat faster.

I'll never forget when I went to see *Titanic* for the first time. Before the movie came out, I had heard the story several times. We even sang this funny little song about it at camp; it included a line like "We all went to the bottom of the sea . . . the captain, octopus, and me."

And then I saw the movie.

I cried for two days. I never sang that stupid song again. When a story gets real, it does something inside of you. When it isn't real, it feels pretend, shallow—you can sing silly songs about it.

After that sticky July night, things got real and everything began to change. My numb, cool soul was full with something tangible— something chaotic and yet trustworthy. The living God had saved me, made a way for me, and then filled me and began to mess with my life and affections. I hadn't walked an aisle or thought especially hard about Jesus. In one moment he did something I could not have done. This movement was not because of the depth of my new faith in that moment; it was a cross. It was the person I could now see who was saving me.

In one moment I was free and safe forever. God moves. God saves.

In that moment God flipped something dead to life. All the Christmases I sang around wreaths holding candles, all the stories and lessons snapped to life because they only make sense in light of this person.

> When a story gets real, it does something inside of you. When it isn't real, it feels pretend, shallow—you can sing silly songs about it.

However, we can believe in Christ and be free and still be stuck. God was my new master, but I didn't know how to shake all the old ones. I knew a lot about God, but I still did not know him. I believed he was big enough to save me forever, but now I would have to grow to believe he was big enough to weave in and out of my every day, leading me, changing me.

But now he was real, and I was his.

# least good

## abandoning pretending

It was a gorgeous day in Dallas, and I was driving to my home after class. I was only a few blocks from the seminary when my phone rang. One of my best friends, Kathryn, was on the other end. Kathryn and I had grown up together, but it wasn't until college that we became inseparable. Our friendship was sealed while driving out to the lake on a beautiful Sunday, right before the end of freshman year. I played some cheesy Christian song on the stereo and the girl broke down, telling me she wanted to live differently—she wanted to live for God. One song and she was changed. Seriously, she never looked back. I love people like that . . . sincere, impassioned, decisive.

Years later, when I answered the phone, she was crying.

"Jennie, do you think my dad is in heaven?"

My heart stopped and my brain raced to find the answer. I scanned through my memories of his mess of a life and found myself doubting.

Kathryn had recently lost her dad to a heart attack. Her dad, Mike, was one of the most joyful, screwed-up men I knew. He had broken his marriage and could be seen more in bars than church. His life did not at all resemble the steadfast Christian men I knew.

But something about Mike was alive and full of joy. Every time you were around him, you felt it. He befriended every person he ever met. In fact, Kathryn had to go to his grocery store and pharmacy and barbershop after he died because he counted them all good friends, and Kathryn knew they would be wondering where he was. The man loved well.

This phone call was one of desperation—Kathryn was not sure her dad was in heaven. The further she dug into her memories of his life, the more destructive his behavior seemed.

Kathryn waited on the other line for my response. I paused and prayed, looking for what to say to my hurting friend.

> On a core level, are we really as "good" as we think we are?

There are a lot of things about God and Christianity that are a worthwhile debate, but the fact that we all sin is typically not one of them. I have never met a person so brave as to say he was perfect, but I have met *a lot* of people who think they are good people.

What do they mean by that? Do they mean they have good motives, do good things? Or do they mean they are just good, like warm chocolate chip cookies are always just good? I get the impression when they say that about themselves, they are saying, "God thinks I am okay."

On a core level, are we really as "good" as we think we are?

Despite my impressive script performance, I've rarely felt deep, deep in my bones as though I'm a truly good person. I didn't perceive myself as being as bad as others, and I worked to maintain the respect of people with my external behavior, but I always knew, even on my best day, how far from good I really was. There has always been a dichotomy inside of me.

A person can learn the right behavior for any character quality. Though some of my behavior came from a pretty sincere place, the truth has always been that without God's intervention, I am selfish and prideful every minute of every day. I care what others think because deep down I want to be seen as great—I want to matter. I find it impossible to forgive; to truly be able to forgive people who hurt us must be one of God's greatest miracles. And I belittle the God of the universe by worrying as if he is not really in control. Inside, my soul seems prone to slant toward every quality I would never want to possess. I live assuming I am not alone in these weaknesses. Mostly because I know a lot of people.

## sandy face

I've always thought the epic war in our universe was pretty simple—good versus bad. But if you read about the war in the Bible, it was always more complicated than that, even from day one. Adam and Eve chose evil, but then they found themselves in a place without church or Bibles or pressure from their priest. On their own intuition, they ran from God and tried to cover themselves and their shame with fig leaves (Gen. 3). These were leaves of pretending, the same leaves we call *religion* or perhaps *morality* or maybe *being good*. They tried to cover up just how bad they were.

I've done this. I do this. I impress the world with passionate, visible morality while avoiding God altogether. There is something to humility that is costly . . . something resembling humiliation . . . an outright declaration of the wreck we are without God rather than composing a beautiful existence that barely needs a savior.

We've often run to pretending, to covering ourselves with religion or the fig leaf of appearing good. It was the biggest fight Christ picked, and yet it is still our biggest problem. We think we can appear okay . . . okay to God and to each other, and that if we construct really pretty coverings out of our leaves, no one will know.

But God is clear. The state of our invisible hearts takes precedence over all the good behavior, over all the bad. From Adam and Eve to the churches described in Revelation, God addresses the inner parts of man. This is what he takes issue with the most.

> God is clear. The state of our invisible hearts takes precedence over all the good behavior, over all the bad.

This took a long time for me to learn because everything in our world works in opposition to this idea. We judge children on their behavior or performance from the time they are born. "Oh, what a good baby," we say. "She is so quiet and eats so well." We issue good grades for good work come kindergarten. We give our kids time-outs when they are bad and a star on their charts when they are good. Then we become adults and we get promotions or awards based on our good performance.

People just flat-out like us better if we are . . . good.

Everything in this life seems to hinge on our external behavior. Being good matters. Quite honestly, it is all we have to go on. We don't, for the most part, work with the invisible space of souls and thoughts and motives and feelings. They're so abstract and immeasurable. And then God showed up in the flesh. Christ appeared and turned our system of being good on its head.

When Jesus came, he went to the most broken, the least good. In fact, it was always the most sinful he ministered to. He touched them and healed them and loved them, and they loved him back. They needed him.

I remember the first time it occurred to me that my life looked more like the lives of the people Jesus rebuked than the people Jesus drew near to. I was reading his words to the religious in Matthew, "So you also outwardly appear righteous to others, but within you are full of hypocrisy and lawlessness" (23:28).

Ugh. I felt that way. I knew deep down I was screwed up. I also knew nobody really knew it, and I liked it that way. I did not want to be facedown in the sand like all the sinners Jesus healed. I wanted to stay bright and shiny and good, and comfortably on my feet. Yet when I read the words of Christ, I felt this call. A call to fall on my face.

> When I read the words of Christ, I felt this call. A call to fall on my face.

It physically hurts to see our pride, to see our sin, to quit playing good, to feel broken and to need God. And it hurts even more to let others see it. So we run from falling; we choose large fig leaves to cover up with and not God. We run from that vulnerable feeling that we may not measure up, all while aching to measure up.

Throughout the history of humanity, this has been how we engage God. First we ask, is he real? And second, do we really need him?

What if the thing we are trying to impress him with was the very thing keeping us from him?

## redefining hands

I love the song "Beautiful Things" by Gungor. It says, "You make beautiful things out of dust. You make beautiful things out of us."

God's people have always been good at running from him. Jeremiah was one of the people God sent to remind them that God was real and that they needed him, and that he wanted them back. So he sent Jeremiah to the home of a potter.

When Jeremiah arrived, the piece of clay in the potter's hands was misshapen and ruined. As Jeremiah watched, the potter reworked the same clay into something beautiful, an altogether different vessel.

As Jeremiah walked away, God asked him, "Can I not do with you as this potter has done? . . . Like the clay in the potter's hand, so you are in my hand" (Jer. 18:5–6).

Christ kept drawing close to broken people while he was here. For the woman caught in adultery, about to be stoned in John 8, her face in the sand, Jesus protected her from stones. And to protect her from eternal judgment, he whispered the same thing that he whispers to us: *Repent, because you are not good; you are not okay. Come back to me. You need me.* He says, *Go and sin no more* (John 8:11), which is impossible apart from the righteousness Christ offers to those who come to him in faith. He is what makes us right.

There is something so beautiful about people aware of their sin and their need for God. That is beautiful to God. He can work with that, enter into that. Jesus' first command after nearly every encounter with a needy person was for them to repent. He promised these broken people hope and healing. He promised to make a way for them. Often, after these encounters, he would turn to the religious people who seemed to have it all together and confront their sin of pride and pretending. Yet with every opportunity, for the most part, they never repented. They thought they were fine without Jesus. They did not need him.

A few years ago we were in San Antonio, enjoying a weekend away as a family. We had spent a day at SeaWorld and the next day on the River Walk. Most of my time was spent chasing our two-year-old and forcing her to hold my hand, mainly so she did not die. Often I found myself saying to her, "Caroline, hold my hand or you will get a time-out." I wanted to control her with that hand, for her protection.

My oldest son, Conner, who was eight at the time, witnessed all of this. Toward the end of our second day together, with Caroline tucked safely in her stroller, I reached out leisurely and affectionately to grab my son's hand. I wanted to walk with him. He pulled his hand back, and immediately I knew why. I thought about what it had meant to hold Mom's hand the last few days . . . a fight, discipline, controlling . . . and I also knew he was getting close to the age where it was no longer cool to need Mom. I knelt down in the center of the walkway on the River Walk. I grabbed both his hands and simply said, "Will you hold my hand just because I love you, just because I am your mom?"

I had to redefine my hand for him. What seemed to be a hand that signaled discipline and failure was about something different; it was about a relationship. I wanted him to love me and need me just because he was eight and I was his mom, not because I was disciplining him or trying to control him.

God is reaching out to us, wanting us to see we need him. But since he is God, we think he wants some song and dance from us—in other words, behavior modification. He actually just wants *us*. He longs to set us free. And yes, to accomplish all that, he wants us entirely.

God is home to us. He is where we were made to be. He is what we were made for. We just forget all that while we are trying to be good and independent.

Pretending to be good halts God's movement in our life. Legalism or religion helps us feel better about ourselves, puffs us up, gives us the posture to be critical and judgmental and prideful. Oh, and everything human about us loves that. It feels better to live that way. It feels better to walk independently and all grown-up, not holding hands with your mom on the River Walk when you want to feel cool and like an adult. We want to not need God.

# forehead smudges

I was visiting a halfway house filled with men who had all recently been released from prison. It was the holidays, and the group I was with had brought them a few insignificant gifts to open around Christmastime. I hadn't known what to expect, but my heart instantly began melting.

I saw an older man with his worn shirt tucked in pouring lemonade—the grainy kind that you add water to and stir—and putting out cookies that looked store-bought but were arranged in a pattern on a plate. The other men greeted us with smiles as if they were welcoming the president. I had rushed to get there that night—I was dealing with sitters and car pools and wrapping gifts—and honestly I felt a little cranky, but at the sight of these humble men my pulse slowed and I didn't want to be anywhere else.

We went around the room, and each man shared a little about his life. With tears and true ownership, each man confessed his weaknesses and mistakes. Their hearts bled for the damage they had brought to those they love, and they gushed at how they lived forgiven because of Christ. There was no air about them, no pretense. Christ had moved into their wrecked lives and restored them. They spoke with peace, and I sensed they possessed hope.

I found myself longing to be like them, these men recovering from the consequences of sin. I wanted to need God as they did and feel broken as they did and be transparent as they were. It was as if they were already exposed . . . already caught. "Screwed up" was written on their foreheads—no need to act like it wasn't. And something about that brought freedom. It made God the hero, not them.

My soul resonated with that. Even though I'm a blonde, mom-of-three pastor's wife connecting with criminals fresh out of prison, I am a human, and we humans arrive with "screwed up" on our foreheads. We come that way, but somewhere between toddlerhood and being a grown-up we learn to wipe off our forehead signs. To sit up straight. To be good.

But before God I am no different from these men. My forehead is clean; my soul certainly is not. That day on an old, beat-up sofa with some old, beat-up guys, I rethought the things I valued in people and the types of people I valued, and I realized that God shone more through those accused and hurting men than through me.

We are all hiding from each other with big fig leaves, but God says, "You could stop because I am a way better covering. I have an actual payment for all the sin you are hiding. But it will take coming out from behind your leaves. It will take humility to see that you need me" (John 11:25, 1 John 1:8, paraphrased). The irony is that Jesus' blood takes the least good and makes them the most good. It's beautiful.

## face to the ground

We don't want to fall. We like to see great testimonies of God's grace, but we don't want to be the testimony.

Even though I was bright and shiny—I was full of sin and pride. Eventually I fell, dramatically, face-first, crying because I had lived like a Pharisee in all my pride and arrogance. I actually have learned to fall a lot. I fall because I can't keep pretending I am okay when I know deep down I'm not. But I also fall because I find God in the sand. I find God with my face in it. And then he gets to be the lifter of my head, rather than my pride.

About the same time my more acceptable sin was bringing me to my face, my friend

Anyone can get to heaven—no matter how messy his or her life. And by the same token, anyone can be kept out—regardless of all his or her fancy goodness.

anything

Kathryn called about her more blatantly sinning father. Everything I had thought God wanted from me was in question. When you strip away the Christians you know, the lessons and songs, preachers and American morality, when you strip away everything you have ever known about God and only look at Jesus, what he did, what he said, who he loved . . . there is only one thing needed. One.

Anyone can get to heaven—no matter how messy his or her life. And by the same token, anyone can be kept out—regardless of all his or her fancy goodness.

I needed to answer Kathryn.

"I know this, Kathryn . . . It is the work of Christ that saves any of us. Our behavior here is really all the same—we all screw it up pretty bad without God. Some of us are just better at covering our sin up. When we get to heaven, a whole heck of a lot of people we never expected are going to be there, and a lot of good people we thought were going to be there won't be. God deals with the heart, the unseen spaces in us, and while your dad never mastered church or his marriage, he had something inside of him that poured out on everyone who came in touch with him. . . . Did he know Jesus?"

Kathryn had never asked her dad where he stood with Jesus Christ, so that night she got on her face and begged God to somehow show her that Mike was in heaven . . . she was desperate and pleading for proof so obvious that it couldn't be denied.

The day after pleading with God and with no knowledge of Kathryn's prayer, her aunt, with whom she had never had a spiritual conversation, reluctantly called. She nervously told Kathryn that a voice that she knew to be God woke her up in the night and told her that Mike was with him, and that Mike had given his heart to Jesus a few years earlier when Kathryn's father-in-law passed. Her aunt hadn't even been at the funeral, but they all agreed, as they thought back, that her dad had experienced a sudden shift toward spiritual things. She remembered that something was different in him following that time—not perfect or "good" or showy, but something deep and real had appeared.

> *How deep the Father's love for us*
> *How vast beyond all measure*
> *That He would give His only Son*
> *To make a wretch His treasure*

> *I will not boast in anything*
> *No gifts, no powers, no wisdom*
> *But I will boast in Jesus Christ*
> *His death and resurrection*

> *Why should I gain from His reward?*
> *I cannot give an answer*
> *But this I know with all my heart*
> *His wounds have paid my ransom*[2]

Grace is scary insane. I remember trembling while reading Chuck Swindoll's *The Grace Awakening*. I was beginning to understand the implications of grace.

> Grace says you have nothing to give, nothing to earn, nothing to pay. You couldn't if you tried! . . . Salvation is a free gift. You simply lay hold of what Christ has provided. Period. And yet the heretical doctrine of works goes on all around the world and always will. It is effective because the pride of men and women is so strong. We simply *have* to *do* something in order to feel right about it. It just doesn't make good humanistic sense to get something valuable for nothing.[3]

In one act God did what no amount of effort on our part could do. He sacrificed his perfect son, placing every sin on him. No sin would

> In one act God did what no amount of effort on our part could do.

be exempt from this ransom. He would pay for every one of them. Every murder, every sexual sin and perversion, every prideful thought, every idol we would worship, every bit of gossip or slanderous word, every time we impatiently snap, every sin that has ever shamed us would be paid . . . for those who would see their sin and turn to Christ for that forgiveness.

It's not just those in prison who are far from God; often it's those of us sitting in pews, deciding where to go to lunch after this guy finishes talking about a God we barely need.

"I will not boast in anything." I'm getting more comfortable with imperfect forehead signs.

Here is mine:

I am crazy screwed up.

And my only hope is my Jesus.

::: 3

# missing buttons
## abandoning shame

We all feel it . . . eventually.

I never spoke out in class; I didn't want the attention. I especially didn't want to get in trouble. Each side of my blonde hair was usually pulled back in a little pink barrette, and I wore knee-high white, thin socks with blue-and-white sneakers that velcroed and had rainbows on them. I loved those shoes. Mrs. Reed was the meanest teacher I'd ever had. All my other teachers had given us hugs and seemed to know how we were feeling, even if we never said. In Mrs. Reed's second-grade classroom, little blue Smurfs lined the wall, each of their white hats displaying a name. Three little magnetic buttons lined their tummies. Real Smurfs didn't have buttons.

The boys always got in trouble, and when they were caught they would take a painful walk in front of the rest of the class to remove buttons from their Smurfs. The first button cost them five minutes of recess. I don't remember what happened when you lost all three; back then they could have probably locked you in a closet or something else just as terrible.

This day, Brent, who wanted to be my boyfriend, was sitting across from me, kicking me under the table. So I kicked him back and told him to stop.

Mrs. Reed looked up from her paper. "Jennie, get a button."

The room started spinning . . . this had never happened to me. And it was one of those times in life you think never will happen to you. I stood up in front of everyone and began the painful walk to strip my Smurf of his pride.

Recess came, and as the class filed out, I stayed glued to my seat for five eternal minutes. I wanted to be under my seat. Mrs. Reed was grading papers and not even looking at me. I was sure she was too disappointed to acknowledge me anymore. I felt as if I were getting a fever. Some disease was spreading through me.

It wasn't the last time I'd have that feeling. Shame seems to fill me sometimes, even now, even while holding on to grace.

## weighty

All kinds of things keep people from God. Even those of us who may appear as though we live extra close to him don't really. Sometimes we are close to him, of course. But lots of times we aren't. We are supposed to want God all the time for everything and trust him with every aspect of our lives. We are also supposed to handwrite thank-you notes and vote in local elections.

But when our sin distances us from God, what do we do? When I sit with one of my kids after he or she repents for lying or clobbering a sibling, never has my child said, "I feel so much better because that sin was really detracting from my prayer life."

We aren't so bothered by what sin and mistakes do to our relationship with God. Maybe he doesn't feel real enough, or maybe we think God just accepts our sin. When we are saved, spiritual things begin working inside us and disrupting the way we used to think and live. Sin becomes distasteful because it fights with who we are. God becomes our chief desire. These are marks that we are believers. Unless there is some craving for God and some distaste for sin in us, we should question if we are believers. We are children of a living God who wants us out of bondage, out of sin, out of the weight of shame.

We are so often content to live stuck. I've seen it in my own life, and I constantly hear it over phone lines and see it in people's eyes—the weight of shame, the horrible feeling dating all the way back to the day I picked a button off my Smurf.

How does all this intersect, this shame and grace and holiness, and this God who requires everything but yet forgives everything?

I grew up thinking that revealing the worst parts of me, especially in church, would be unacceptable. If grace is real, how could I ever feel that? The places that hold grace should be the safest places to unveil our humanity.

But they usually aren't. The gospel of grace fights every piece of pride in us. When God gives us grace, he is also taking something from us. He takes our control.

> We are supposed to want God all the time for everything and trust him with every aspect of our lives. We are also supposed to handwrite thank-you notes and vote in local elections.

So many of us don't live in grace even though we may have grown up singing about it since birth.

We want to earn the feeling that we are okay. We want to climb ladders and have everyone tell us how proud they are and how much we deserve everything good, so we can nod and smile as we agree. If

> When God gives us grace, he is also taking something from us. He takes our control.

we are really extra bad, like the prostitute or the men just out of prison, grace is the best thing we've ever heard of. But for the good kids with most of our buttons on our Smurfs, it feels a little different to think we may need God in a desperate way.

True grace threatens our control. But it gives something too. It gives something better.

## inside anchors

Heather's eyes always carried that look, the look that said she didn't deserve to be talking to you. It was something she often hid with an edge of a personality that usually pushed people away. She had actually tried several times to push me away. I would either chuckle at her and ignore it or tell her to get over whatever she was acting mad about.

As close as we had been for years, I'd never been able to figure out that look, the one under her tougher, cooler exterior.

Heather came over one day with her head down. She had something to tell me. She worked to get the words out. She'd had an abortion while she was in college and now, finally, she was stepping out of the darkness of hiding. She had never told anyone until a few weeks before. Now she wanted a few close friends to know.

I barely caught a glimpse of her eyes that day. But I listened. I told her I loved her and nothing she was telling me was changing the way I felt about her, that God's grace was enough for this, as devastating as it was. But from the glimpse I stole of her eyes, I knew she didn't believe me.

Shame had been an anchor tied to her insides—she had been carrying it completely alone, crushed with fear that if she told, if anyone knew, it would change everything.

I think even those of us who appear bright and shiny feel a little twinge of this kind of shame. I think we all do. Even if we call ourselves good, deep down somewhere we know we are not. Darker, more disconcerting things sit just under everything nice about us.

Paul says, "I know that nothing good dwells in me, that is, in my flesh. For I have the desire to do what is right, but not the ability to carry it out" (Rom. 7:18). If nothing good lives in us, how can anyone feel self-righteous? We should all be safe before each other if we are all equally messed up. But we don't feel safe—because it is not safe. People judge, especially those who claim Jesus.

Often when I go to be alone with God—to really meet God, not just say a quick prayer or read some verses—I feel as if I can't. I feel as though I would rather be anywhere but there. And I think other people feel that way too. I know good and well that God sees my sin, my junk, and that is not comfortable or easy to reconcile. So often I will say a prayer and read my verses and go along my way. And inside I am like King David in the Bible, after he had committed adultery and murder: "When I kept silent, my bones wasted away through my groaning all day long. For day and night your hand was heavy upon me" (Ps. 32:3-4). Even our bones hurt from the weight of sin.

> I know good and well that God sees my sin, my junk, and that is not comfortable or easy to reconcile.

But what if I am approaching it all wrong? What if the way I felt after removing that button, or the way my friend felt telling me her darkest secret, or how I want to bolt when I get before God . . . what if we were actually misinterpreting the feeling?

Every person reading this in some way is broken, imperfect. Some of the brokenness is hurt from our past, some of the brokenness is our own fault, and some of it is just the sad state of our planet. But we all feel it.

But what I feel when I see God needs to be defined and sorted through or it will keep me always running from him. What is weight designed to do? God created the cosmos and the rules by which it functions. What is the purpose of weight? Anything without weight evaporates or lifts. Something weightless rises.

Weight causes things on earth to fall—to remain grounded. What if the weight of sin holds the same purpose as physical weight?

When I curl up on my sofa with God and his Word, that feeling that makes me want to bolt should be the feeling that keeps me there with him. It's the weight of my sin pushing me down from the high and lofty places where my pride would rather keep me. See, I like to feel good about myself. I prefer high places where I am numb to a place where my face is wet from tears because I realize how hopeless I am apart from Jesus. I want to be poised and together and cute and happy. That's the girl I want to be. But my sin . . . I don't want to deal with that. I often live padded with self-righteousness.

> The weight of my sin grounds me. Breaks me. Shows me I need Jesus.

The weight of my sin grounds me. Breaks me. Shows me I need Jesus. Without this need for God, I would never go to him. But even those of us who feel weighed down don't go to Jesus or even the church or other believers with the weight of our sin. We hide because the very place that promises grace can feel condemning. But sin and shame never get lighter. In fact, I've only ever seen them grow bigger and heavier when left alone.

In the months that followed Heather's confession of having had an abortion, I watched as she faithfully and painfully pursued God, healing, and forgiveness. Heather found herself in a community where grace is not just sung—it is practiced. We have seen friends come out of hiding, confessing broken marriages, pornography addictions, depression, abuse, alcoholism, fear, even self-righteousness, and they've been met with the restorative grace of God.

Heather's eyes changed as her anchor grew smaller and she was consistently met with love and grace that comes because of the blood of Jesus. What a lie she believed for decades—that revealing the broken pieces of her would push people away, push God away!

## bolt or stay

Even if we find gracious people, are we safe? While Jesus was here he spent his time with the most broken people. The put-together, bright-and-shiny people would ask, "Why does he eat with tax collectors and sinners?" (Mark 2:16). And Jesus would answer them, "Those who are well have no need of a physician, but those who are sick. I came not to call the righteous, but sinners" (Mark 2:17).

As I said, I believe the weight we feel was meant to remind us we are all in the latter category. We are all sinners in need of repentance. That ache and weight is pushing us to our knees, begging us to repent and look to God for forgiveness.

So why don't we go to God? Why do we bolt instead of stay?

Sometimes we bolt because we hate to repent. It feels like death to confess. But when God calls us to something that feels backward, it is usually his path to our freedom. The path out of shame is to see our sin and turn from it toward our God. And there we find peace and a God who can say, *I can take care of this . . . Actually it's already been taken care of.*

The disease that began with my Smurf buttons would grow and grow. I spent most of my life sick with the feeling that I wasn't measuring up. Every once in a while, even now, the same feeling I felt for those five eternal minutes in second grade creeps in, like I'm in trouble with the teacher.

"For freedom Christ has set us free; stand firm therefore, and do not submit again to a yoke of slavery" (Gal. 5:1). For freedom . . . but are we truly free?

Freedom isn't found in rebelling or pretending. Both places bind us tighter. Freedom is found in a person who took care of the buttons we are missing, the places that are scarred in us and stolen from us.

When David finally went to God, everything changed. "I acknowledged my sin to you. Blessed is the one whose transgression is forgiven, whose sin is covered. Blessed is the man against whom the Lord counts no iniquity" (Ps. 32:1, 5).

If I view God rightly, I run to him the second any weight descends on my shoulders. He deals with it. I go to him broken, like the adulterous woman in the Bible, and he takes my hand and helps me up and says to me as he said to her, "Neither do I condemn you; go, and from now on sin no more" (John 8:11).

> Freedom is found in a person who took care of the buttons we are missing, the places that are scarred in us and stolen from us.

And with that taste of freedom, with that taste of forgiveness, I want to run from my sin and toward a God who loves me.

Romans 2:4 says, "God's kindness is meant to lead you to repentance." Sometimes, when we sit down on our couches with God, we're afraid he's the mean teacher from second grade, when instead he is the safest place we'll ever be. His presence is the only place where invisible weight is lifted. The only place where hidden, broken spaces are mended. The only place where we are defined apart from our successes and our failures.

This is the gospel:

*[We] all have sinned and fall short of the glory of God* (Rom. 3:23).

*And then God did what the law, could not do. He sent his own Son in the likeness of sinful flesh and for sin, he condemned sin in the flesh* (Rom. 8:3, paraphrased).

Christ did what none of us, no matter how bright and shiny, could do. We get to be free.

# giant people
## abandoning approval

It was pretty late. Most of the lights were out. I had gotten tied up with friends and packing and forgotten that my parents kept 10:00 p.m. bedtimes. But they were still up waiting for their oldest daughter, the first one to have left the nest—a freshman now at the University of Arkansas—to come home for the weekend.

This night I went into their room and sat on the corner of their bed, home from college with something important to talk about. I am sure that night I looked to them like their little girl who hadn't really grown up that much, like I might be asking if I could go to a dance with a cute boy or spend the evening out with a friend.

But I wasn't asking to go to a dance.

After the wooden crosses at camp, God kept getting bigger to me. God was real and speaking and moving in me. I was hearing him and

God was real and speaking and moving in me. I was hearing him and obeying—but was I obeying him in every way, no matter the cost?

obeying—but was I obeying him in every way, no matter the cost? Was I willing to do anything he asked?

When God began awakening in me, he started awakening me for the things of him. I wanted to be about building his kingdom, not only at the University of Arkansas but throughout the world. I was feeling led overseas. It was not clear where, but I could go for a year or two and serve through a ministry I was involved with in college.

As I sat on their bed I told them, "Mom and Dad, I feel like God is calling me to go overseas. I don't know all the details, but I feel sure of this calling in me." I looked at them expectantly, waiting to hear what they had to say.

## streams and rivers

Every conscious person has thoughts, feelings, and passions streaming through him or her. These streams never stop, and they're rarely filtered. They flood us with messages, and out of those thoughts we live, we make decisions, we create—we even regress as a direct result of these streams moving to and from our hearts and minds.

The obvious streams are our preoccupation with food or sex, or more likely, returning e-mails or building grocery lists. But the deeper streams, the ones that control our lives, those are where we doubt and dream and feel afraid or insecure. Typically we just leave them all there, streaming through us, controlling us.

God often speaks of the heart, or our souls. Nothing about me matters more than my heart, so why can't I seem to control my heart or even locate it? For most of my life it seems to have had its own way, navigated by fear or desire. It moves and it ends up moving me.

I know my heart is tangibly real in this sense—I see evidence of its affections. But how does one control the heart?

Ever since I was young, I have been fascinated by the life of King David. He made so many terrible mistakes, and yet he bled God. He was passionate. Over and over again throughout his journaling through Psalms, he says variations of this phrase: "The LORD is on my side; I will not fear. What can man do to me?" (Ps. 118:6).

And his life flowed out of this mentality. Because he feared and adored God, he feared nothing else. No one else. What was different about my faith than David's? Why did I live with this stream of fear of people?

The current running through my heart was no little creek—it was a frantic river drowning out my God and controlling my heart and thus my life. I loved God, but I loved un-invisible people more. I worshipped them. I bowed down for their gold stars, especially from the two people I found myself looking at that night on the corner of their bed.

> I loved God, but I loved un-invisible people more.

I grew up knowing the facts about God, and one of those facts was that he wanted to possess my heart completely. That I would love the Lord, my God, with my all my heart, soul, mind . . . that all of me would love him the most (Deut. 6:5). But I couldn't live it then. I was busy making most everyone in my life happy, and it was working for me—at least most of the time. I'm lying. It wasn't working. I was completely wrecked inside. How does anyone ever make everyone happy? I waited for my parents' answer.

※ ※
※ ※

Was I the only one torn like this? In love with God and yet eagerly serving everybody but him?

I wouldn't call my friend Julie afraid. No one would ever call her a people pleaser. She always speaks her mind. We've often gotten in fights after she tears through a sensitive subject with a lot of human casualties. I've always admired her though; she's so different from me. She's seemingly unaware of everyone's judgments or criticisms of her unruly personality. She just bleeds confidence.

But I know Julie. Julie is afraid. She just protects herself differently than I do. I think we all care on some level what others think. If we do not desire the acceptance of those we love, we are barely human. It is one of the attributes that defines us—our desire to be accepted first by God and then by others. Most people don't need everybody to be happy with them. But everybody wants somebody to be happy with them.

That night on my parents' bed, as I told them I wanted to obey God by serving him in another country, far from their categories and dreams, many streams flooded me. They were streams that, at the time, trumped the planet-building God.

My parents weren't wrong to express their opinions. I was only eighteen, and I was their daughter. They never said I was forbidden to go. But I was intuitive. I could feel it. I could feel their disapproval.

So I didn't go. I didn't even think about going anymore.

In the decade that followed, as much as my love and understanding of God grew, this river of idolatry only rushed stronger and stronger, oftentimes making me anxious, even frantic. Since the invisible thoughts of people are not easily controlled, I would spin, longing to control them.

People had to shrink for me before God had me completely . . . but how?


## scary quiet

When you close your eyes and everything gets scary quiet, you hear your heart. It's always there, of course. But you never hear its streams and rivers moving through you until it gets uncomfortably quiet.

When I get still and hear the loudest thing in me, it is often that I am chasing everyone but God. And I fear if he gets too close, he'll see it. But if I let him close anyway, we sit together on days like that, looking over the frantic river that is wearing me out. He never says, *I told you so*. He could, but he never does.

Love is jealous . . . especially God's love. He wants me, and I want everybody else.

God knows we all have this problem, loving everybody but him. So he called a prophet to dedicate his days to answering the same question I ask: how do we stop chasing everybody else and come back to God?

> Love is jealous . . . especially God's love. He wants me, and I want everybody else.

God told his servant Hosea to go into town and take a prostitute as his wife. God saw Israel pursuing every idol but him— similar to my ways—and this was his way of talking to Israel about it. Hosea obeyed and married the prostitute Gomer. Together they had several children, and though Hosea was a loving, gracious husband and provided all she needed, Gomer kept going back to other lovers who abused her and never loved her back. The streams of her heart were nearly drowning her.

As I started reading Hosea, though, I thought its purpose was to display God's wrath—his anger with Israel . . . with me. He did start off pretty ticked. He said things like, "I will no more have mercy on the house of Israel . . . You are not my people and I am not your God" (Hos. 1:6, 9).

But then, in the midst of this dramatic metaphor, God says about those of us chasing other loves,

> *Therefore, behold, I will allure her,*
> *and bring her into the wilderness,*
> *and speak tenderly to her.*

*And there I will give her her vineyards*
*and make the Valley of Achor a door of hope.*
*And there she shall answer as in the days of her youth,*
*as at the time when she came out of the land of Egypt.*

*And in that day, declares the LORD, you will call me "My Husband," and no longer will you call me "My Baal." For I will remove the names of the Baals from her mouth, and they shall be remembered by name no more.* (Hos. 2:14–17)

Every time I sit by the banks of my sin and my other loves, right as I think he is about to wipe me out because my heart feels so out of control, he steps into the river and redirects it. "The king's heart is a stream of water in the hand of the LORD; he turns it wherever he will" (Prov. 21:1). It is only God who moves my heart. He chases me down and lures me back to him; while I am running to everyone else, he runs after me. God brings me back to the place where it fares well with me, reminding me he is my husband. There is no spinning, no fear, only perfect acceptance and peace.

> I can let other people down. If God is for me . . . the God of the universe for me . . . who could be against me? Whom else do I fear?

I can let other people down. If God is for me . . . the God of the universe for me . . . who could be against me? Whom else do I fear?

When God became real to me in high school, I came home from the crosses at camp and gathered an assortment of younger girls so we could talk about him. I don't remember thinking I was supposed to do that. After I fell in love with God and was filled with his Spirit, I just did it. I started gushingly teaching everything I knew about him.

I've lived since then with a very clear sense of what he wants me to do, and usually it's to talk about him in some form. His gifts in my life were never a secret to me or those who saw them used. As he did with every believer, he gave me something to make him bigger.

When I would speak or even write, I was on display—and being on display would at times make me physically ill. I simply could not handle people's invisible thoughts about me, or at times their very visible criticism. I dreaded it more than facing God and telling him that I had sat on every gift he had given me. So I would teach, but I always held back. I always kept the pulse of how I was being received, and I agonized to the point of paralysis when it was negative. I was like a politician worried about the polls.

Rather than dying to my need for approval, I died to the clear callings God had put in my soul and the clear gifts and equipping he had given me. I just wished it all away . . . it was costing too much. It was costing me my people, everyone's approval, the thing I loved most. So I sat on it. The little portion of his work that God gave me to do for a few years before I see him again, I sat on, praying it would go away. I was no different than Jonah running from God's clear call to share him with Nineveh. I was not going. I'm thankful he didn't have me eaten by a whale.

I did wonder sometimes, when I closed my eyes and let it get scary quiet, if I was missing the best things, the things that matter most, because I was afraid.

He knows we keep chasing other loves until we love him most. We keep spinning. We keep searching, restless. We keep missing all he has for us. He'll always feel far away, drowned out by other louder rivers, until every other thing fades away and he becomes the only thing.

:: 5

# normal drug
## abandoning entitlement

It was our first date. Zac was unusually cute in his plaid button-up with the sleeves casually rolled up, but it still did not occur to me that I could be eating across from the man I would eat with forever. We had met that summer at a camp where we both were counselors, the same camp where I had come face-to-face with Jesus a few years earlier. I remember cutting my chicken on that date. It was hard to eat because he kept asking me questions, but I was managing.

He asked me what I wanted most in life. It was a great first-date question.

I did not even have to think about it. At that point, my life had flipped toward God. He was incredibly real to me, so I naively but passionately said, "I just don't want to be normal."

I realize now that I'd been watching all the families I knew and,

41

I am sure, feeling like a hippie felt in the sixties. I wanted something radical. I had no idea what, but something not normal. I wanted more. Well, Zac loved my answer and drove back up eleven hours to see me again a few weeks later. I married that cute boy, and we started trying to build our not-normal lives together.

For a while we felt kind of different. We were young and passionate and adventurous until a few years passed and I took a pregnancy test, and then life changed. Normal felt like a necessity—a mortgage and health insurance and a safe house with a cute nursery. Normal started looking good.

Before our first son was born, we moved closer to family. As I sat with one of my friends from college who was also pregnant with her first, we talked about college and God. We talked about how passionate we had been, how single-mindedly sold out. I said, "I want to stay that way. I don't want to get numb, and yet I feel myself caring so much more about what stroller to buy than about heaven."

She replied, "I don't think it will ever be like college again. We will always look back on those days as our most sold out."

I was terrified she was right.

I knew that what was happening was common. As real life and responsibilities pressed in, I felt God being pressed out. Religion, church, and Bible study were all in place—but truly surrendered lives, the kind God could use anywhere and in any way he chose, had quickly turned into planned and calculated lives that focused on things like saving for a Suburban or minivan. But was that the way God planned for lives to be lived—people selling out to him in college or at some point later, only to fondly look back on the glory days while they get on with their expected and ordinary lives?

> As real life and responsibilities pressed in, I felt God being pressed out.

There had to be more. But there wasn't much time to think

about it—I was due with our first baby and we were looking for our first house and choosing bedding for the nursery. And otherwise, all was well with my soul. To abandon normal seemed scary and uncomfortable, even unreasonable.

Couldn't I have both? More of God *and* the life I wanted? I felt him waiting while I headed into my own little experiment to try.

## lattes and lawns

Not long after we settled in our first house and the baby was born, I went walking with a sweet friend, Aimee, a new mom as well. We had grown up in similar ways, with most of our needs and even our desires met. And I think even the goals we had for our kids at that point were similar—to live near our families, choose a great school with best friends for them, and make some memories together.

As we walked around the neighborhood, it became obvious that Aimee was worked up, even teary. She was broken about this new-found conviction she felt. She wanted more. She believed that her heart had become "entitled." I was struck by the word. I was afraid I was about to come across the first roadblock in my plan . . . my plan to have it all and God too.

She talked about her expectations of a cute house, a safe school, and good friends. And while those weren't bad things, she wondered if those expectations had come from God. Or were we just living, expecting all of it to be there for us? Had our hearts become demanding? If God did not give us and our kids a safe and comfortable life, was he holding out on us?

I knew she was right. Our first little house was located near my parents and only a few blocks from my best friends from college. The nursery was painted to match the bedding, and my little baby boy had enough gear to care for five kids. I was on my way to the dream, but I felt the numb God-distance creeping in like a cancer. What if the things I thought he wanted for me, once again, were the very things keeping me from him?

Before we go on, I should divulge just a little of our current life. I am sitting at my desk in a warm, lovely office in a home that we own—or at least that we make payments to eventually own. I am wearing a North Face fleece and I even have a real, live flower, a white orchid, on my desk—a luxury even in America. (We'll see if I can keep it alive.) I am sipping Starbucks—the high-maintenance kind with multiple flavors and whipped cream—and outside sits a decent-sized SUV that requires a lot of gas. My kids have a Wii and a trampoline.

> It is too easy in this country for blessings to become rights, for stuff and money to become what calls the shots in our lives. And before we know it, God's gifts have replaced God himself.

Surrender is a process for us. In the years since we completely gave ourselves over to God, our lives have changed drastically, but so far we have not moved and sold all we own and given the money to the poor. (We're thinking about it, but we'll get to that later.)

I can't talk about this subject without some transparency. I can't mislead you into thinking that in order to surrender to God completely you must sell all material possessions or houses or SUVs. But I do want to expose the protected bubble of expectations we have built. Money and a good latte protect us from a lot of things. It is too easy in this country for blessings to become rights, for stuff and money to become what calls the shots in our lives. And before we know it, God's gifts have replaced God himself.

But what is normal, really?

If we pull back from our culture for a moment, we realize that the majority of people are dying today because they do not have clean water to drink . . . while I am watering my grass so the neighbors won't frown. And even those of us who are struggling to make ends meet—let's say your family's annual income is $30,000—are still in the top 1 percent of the world's richest people.

Soon after Aimee and I walked together down the lane in front of my new house, I went home to my husband, who was climbing the corporate ladder with very little joy or passion, and told him I was willing to follow him and leave my family and the new painted nursery and my best friends . . . if God called us to something else. A few months later Zac came to me, feeling a tug to pursue ministry, and a few months after that the house was on the market.

I was certainly not willing to do *anything* then, but I can say a lot died for me. It was another step in letting go—a step in dying to my picture of normal, my picture of a perfect nursery and a perfect life.

Little deaths always feel like big deaths until you let go. After you let go you wonder, what was the big deal?

## jenga lives

Because of training and ministry and God's leading, Zac and I moved, and moved some more. And because of all of these moves, I longed to settle again. We had darling little rental houses. We loved each one of them. They were simple—no extra maintenance bills or landscaping. But I was anxious, and I still couldn't let go of an idea in my head of life and how it should look for us. Curtains hanging in a window became a symbol of stability for me. It wasn't the actual curtains; it was a deeper desire to belong somewhere, for my family to dig roots. Through those years we were safe and healthy and happy, and yet I would look side to side, constantly redefining my expectations—and all my friends who represented that for me had curtains in the settled homes they owned.

People, stuff, perfectly crafted houses and lives were never meant to help what hurts. In fact, the more we build everything just right, the more protective we get of it. Like when my kids and I play Jenga. We will get that tower of blocks so high that it's barely hanging on. I know it's bound to fall, but I still want to punch the kid who brings it down. Of course, sometimes it's my fault, but not usually. We have all worked so hard to build it. We build it knowing it will fall, and yet something in me still gets so mad when it does.

There is another normal—it is invisible and lasts forever and it doesn't fall down.

> There is another normal—it is invisible and forever and it doesn't fall down.

The ironic thing about believing in God and supernatural things is that the invisible stuff is actually the most trustworthy, the most stable. So the concrete things we can see and touch, they become the wind, they become the things we try to catch, and over and over, they pass through our fingers and souls, keeping us empty. But when I take my empty self to God, he feels familiar and stable and more like concrete than wind.

Michelle and her husband joined our church shortly after it started, jumping in with everything they had. She e-mailed and asked if we could grab lunch. As we sat across from each other, I could see the heaviness in her eyes. Michelle and her husband had been trying to get pregnant for a long time. She was aching. As many of her friends went through multiple pregnancies, she sat watching and waiting. We talked about God and unfulfilled dreams and wrestled with the unsettling fact that God makes babies and yet, for some reason, he wasn't giving them one. But I sensed there was something under all the pain, something she wasn't saying.

I asked her, "What is the hardest part, Michelle?"

She got quiet, as if to consider how much she should reveal.

Something had been gnawing at her for a while, and it was more than the ache for a child, although that was certainly present.

"I just feel so different from everyone, from all my friends moving on with their lives."

This different feeling, this different path God had for her and her husband was extra difficult because it was *different*. She was hurting and felt alone in her life.

What is it about norms, about sameness, that feels so good? There are, of course, rebels who would rather die than be the same as anyone else, but deep down most of us feel most safe, most at home, with people to whom we are similar. We like our people, and honestly we were designed to be in deep with them—with other humans, running beside them, leaning on them and with them leaning on us.

But God often seems unconcerned with helping us maintain same, simple lives where everything fits and works. I don't know what God's plans are for you, but I do know that we don't hear from him until certain things die. He doesn't compete. And when he does speak, it typically costs something.

Somehow I thought most of my life following God was not supposed to be too costly. Following God is flat costly. It always has been. It doesn't make sense to us, but since this life, these few years, are not the climax from God's perspective, he's okay throwing a little wrench into the short plans we have to be normal here.

## fur coats

Watching a person live recklessly and radically for God resonates deeply with someone who does not know God. Something about that life just feels appropriate—to live based on what we believe. That's refreshing. People who believe in living forever with their God don't totally love this earth. We may feel very different from those who don't believe, but we'll find that they are intrigued, as long as we don't judge them or keep them at arm's length because they live differently. But I'll tell you who we mess with when we live radically: It's not the pagans; it's the Christians. When we actually believe in heaven and hell and angels and a radical God, and we *act* like it . . . it's other Christians who stare shocked and start questioning our sanity.

The Chronicles of Narnia books so move me. Nothing else I have read draws out such a display of two existing universes running side by side like these stories do. C. S. Lewis drew these universes, Narnia and our world, as realities that carry on simultaneously. The great hero in the stories is Aslan, the lion who represents Christ, but in *The Lion, The Witch and the Wardrobe* the human heroine is the youngest of the Pevensie children, Lucy. She is the heroine simply because she believes. God is calling us to this alternate universe, as Lucy was—to push through the fur coats in the closet to get to Narnia and Aslan. He wants to press us through our doubts so we can see the other eternal story going on, of which we are actually a crucial part.

> God wants to press us through our doubts so we can see the other eternal story going on, of which we are actually a crucial part.

It is going on now—angels and God and heaven and us—and I wish that would become our normal. That it would be our reality. I know it is mysterious, but if we confess a belief in God, we are also confessing that all the invisible things, such as angels and heaven and forever, are all real and happening. But it seems as though we try not to think about it most of the time. We rarely even think about God apart from how he could fix us or help us keep up our wobbly Jenga lives.

Not that he minds helping us; he wants us to need him. But from his perspective in eternity, I imagine he is thinking, *If she would just lift her head a little and look up and out, her problems would get smaller and forever with me would get bigger.*

# normal drug

As my friend Aimee and I pushed our strollers outside my safe comfy house, she was feeling discontent with a life spent pining for the perfect school and cute house in a safe neighborhood. She wanted more. She wanted to tell God she would give it all up for him, for any life he had for her, rather than fighting for the normal one she'd wanted. At the time she had no picture of what it would be . . . just a prayer asking God to be God and her promise that she would follow.

Aimee and I talked recently while her husband and oldest daughter were in Haiti helping with recovery efforts. We talked about God and life and giving ourselves away. She called me from Memphis, where they have helped start a church that is part of reconciling a racially divided city. They live in the inner city, hours from her family, with their three beautiful girls in a small house where gunshots can be heard fairly frequently. They don't have the perfect school or house or really anything.

They are displaying the gospel, and there is nothing normal about their lives. And every time I get off the phone with her, all I want is to have nothing normal about our lives. She still bleeds God, and her life is being poured out on the neediest and the most broken. She traded entitlement for surrender, and God took her up on it.

What if heaven and God and forever became our normal?

Wouldn't that change everything?

:: 6

# scrapbooks
## abandoning fear

"Today I started a scrapbook," Alex told me excitedly as we sat talking on the phone about God and the future. She had a lot of future ahead. Alex was nineteen and a sophomore at the University of Texas. Her blonde ringlets must have bounced as she talked, and I imagined her having an expression and posture similar to a five-year-old asking her mom for a Popsicle.

She went on, "I started a scrapbook today describing all I hope for, so I can picture it. I just started cutting out the things that I want: a white, two-story house; a black Volvo SUV; even a cute husband and a number of cute kids."

I sat speechless, trying not to laugh. I knew this was a girl who adored God and sincerely knew him. And while I had never known anyone to be so bold as to build an actual scrapbook, I thought to myself, *I have one of those. We all have one.*

51

anything

We all have the pictures of our lives in our minds, how they "should be," how we hope they will be—how we picture them. We collect these pictures in powerful scrapbooks that exist in our heads. We plan it all out:

- when we will be married;
- how many kids we will have;
- where we will live;
- how much money we will make;
- what our jobs will be;
- what our houses will look like;
- how our husbands will treat us;
- the places we will travel;
- who our friends will be;
- how our kids will behave;
- how close our grandkids should live;
- when we will retire;
- and what our ministries will be like.

> The idea that we would actually hand it all over to God and say, "Go. Build it. Do whatever you want with all I have" . . . it is terrifying.

At some point we realize it doesn't work that way. We can't control the actual scrapbooks—the ones reflecting the past rather than the future. But we still long to try to control our lives and to build them to match the pictures of the lives we want.

And letting go? The idea that we would actually hand it all over to God and say, "Go. Build it. Do whatever you want with all I have" . . . it is terrifying.

What if God has planned any of these as part of the story?

- singleness
- struggle
- adoption
- a difficult husband
- infertility
- moving from the town we love
- an apartment instead of a house
- cancer
- disapproval
- death
- dangerous overseas missions
- financial hardship

What if he lets me suffer? What if he asks me to sacrifice? What if none of my dreams come true?

The very thought of doing *anything* demands everything. We have to face our fears. If we believe he is real, if we believe he has an eternal heart, we have to face the fact that a God like that may mess with our temporary comfort and fictional scrapbooks.

> The very thought of doing *anything* demands everything.

## crazy africa

My friend Natalie and I sat quietly studying the menus. Natalie and I met at church. She lives passionately and always wants to change the world. I love being around dreamers like that. Natalie was the reason I fell in love with Africa—she is so in love with Africa herself that just being near her infects you with that joy.

Natalie always knew exactly what she wanted, so it didn't take long until she was ready to order. I finally closed my menu, and she threw her hands together like a starting gun, eager to listen and talk through the inner workings of our souls.

It didn't take long to get to the subject she and I often wove our way toward . . . singleness. Natalie, now in her mid-thirties, longs to be married. But she isn't, and sometimes, almost like a storm, the feelings of helplessness and desire roll in. So much about Natalie defines her more than her marital status. She travels the world with her job, passionately building and serving a ministry in Africa. When she is home, she sacrificially loves and serves the rest of us.

But that night, it felt to her as though everyone was moving forward with their lives but her. Many of her friends were working on their second or third kid, and she felt left behind, aching for companionship, for her best friend to be running beside her. As we toyed with chips in salsa, the storm rolled in.

"What does God want from me?"

As I watched her fighting for contentment, for peace with things out of her control, my heart fell. I know God's arm . . . and it is unable to be twisted. Yet the desperate feeling of helplessness had her pinned against a wall, and she felt that God was the one holding her there.

Why? Why did it feel like everyone else's husbands were stepping in and Natalie's wasn't? Was God holding out on her?

Seven years ago, one of my best friends, Karen, walked into her bathroom to find her husband on the floor, dead. Her two-year-old daughter stood crying at the door as she did her best to resuscitate him, all the while screaming out to God to bring him back.

A few weeks ago Karen and I had coffee and we talked about this book, this prayer for God to take anything. In the same honest manner that made her one of my closest friends, she confessed, "Jennie, I can't pray that. I can't turn this life over to God. I am scared of what may happen."

My heart sank then too. I knew praying such a prayer was costly, but I never considered that it could mean death. From Karen's perspective, to give God everything meant that he might just take it . . . everything.

I understood why Karen was torn before him. What if his plan for her life included more tragedy? Of course she was afraid.

Karen is remarried, and her beautiful daughter is nine years old now and has a new baby brother and sister. Life has moved on, but the pain of that loss won't go away. And there is no bow to tie this story up. She still aches from the loss of her first husband.

Stories like this expose our deepest fears. What are you most afraid of? What would be the very worst thing that God may allow you to suffer? We all would say his character is loving and good, but do we really trust that he won't get crazy and dish out the same life he gave Job?

> What are you most afraid of? What would be the very worst thing that God may allow you to suffer?

God allowed Satan to take everything from Job but his life because Job feared God more than anyone. Did you hear that? He suffered most *because* he feared God most. And then, for thirty-six chapters in the book of Job, everyone, including Job himself, conjectured about why God would allow this godly man to suffer. *Why is this happening to me?* This sounds terribly familiar to questions in my own head.

But God replied to Job,

> *"Where were you when I laid the foundation of the earth?*
>    *Tell me, if you have understanding.*
> *Who determined its measurements—surely you know!*
> *Or who stretched the line upon it?*

*On what were its bases sunk,*
*    or who laid its cornerstone,*
*    when the morning stars sang together*
*    and all the sons of God shouted for joy?*
*"Or who shut in the sea with doors*
*    when it burst out from the womb,*
*    when I made clouds its garment*
*    and thick darkness its swaddling band,*
*    and prescribed limits for it*
*    and set bars and doors,*
*    and said, 'Thus far shall you come, and no farther,*
*    and here shall your proud waves be stayed'?"* (Job 38:4–11)

God is saying, *I am God! I know what I am doing. I know this feels excruciating, but I am about something here, and I am asking you to trust the one who tells the ocean where to stop and the sun when to launch.*

There is no escaping it. He is God, and if our suffering brings him the most glory, let it be.

> He is God, and if our suffering brings him the most glory, let it be.

Easy to preach, difficult to live.

Recently I studied the life of Mary, the mother of Christ, with women all in the midst of life changes. Each of us was carrying a burden; each of us was a little afraid of what God may do with us. As we studied the life of this woman, our perspectives lifted.

We read about the angel who came to announce the highest calling given to a human. But the high calling was a costly calling, and it came with tremendous suffering. Mary faced the rejection of her fiancé, persecution from her community because of a seemingly illegitimate pregnancy, the pressure of raising the son of God, and ultimately the pain of watching him die a humiliating and excruciating death. All of this lay ahead of her that day the angel came, and the first words out of her mouth were, "Behold, I am the servant of the Lord; let it be to me according to your word" (Luke 1:38).

Let it be as you say.

God, I want to live that way.

## anything but

I often hear this objection to abandoning everything: "What if God calls me to go to Africa or something as sacrificial as that?" To me, there is something mysteriously troubling and intriguing in Africa. It represents everything we are not in America. They are suffering and yet content. Hungry and yet grateful. Broken and yet strong. This represents everything we live afraid of losing.

Something about Africa exposes our little gods. The thought of leaving America and all it offers can show us what we love more than God. So, am I willing to do something as reckless as going to Africa? I believe that being willing to abandon everything requires being willing to go anywhere—and willing to let go of everything.

By its very definition *abandonment* is unreservedly costly:

**a·ban·don** *v.* — **1.** to leave completely and finally; forsake utterly. **2.** to give up the control of. **3.** to yield (oneself) without restraint or moderation. **4.** to surrender one's claim to, right to, or interest in. **5.** to give up entirely.

Are we truly willing to completely and finally forsake this life? To yield ourselves to God without restraint?

If *anything* has "buts," it wouldn't be *anything*. When we look at the God of the universe, who willingly sent his son to be brutally murdered so that *we* get to live in his kingdom forever as his own kids . . . saying that you will do anything *"but"* just doesn't go over well.

We live in a culture that suggests that we deserve certain

things—of course, we can't totally help it, since we were all born here and hardly know any other way. But as believers in a heaven and a God who gave up his son for us, we know there *is* another way, a ridiculous desertion of our plans and of the rights we think we are owed. It feels impossible that the hard things God has put in our lives are really just "light momentary affliction [that] is preparing for us an eternal weight of glory beyond all comparison" (2 Cor. 4:17). The only thing that could get us through, the only thing that could give us perspective, is to "look not to the things that are seen but to the things that are unseen. For the things that are seen are transient, but the things that are unseen are eternal" (v. 18).

> If *anything* has "buts," it wouldn't be *anything*.

God is an anchor in the midst of the difficult chaos of this world. The chaos will be resolved. It will. As Oswald Chambers said, "Faith is deliberate confidence in the character of God whose ways you may not understand at the time."[4]

But it is so hard, isn't it? To dream about heaven, to hope in an invisible God?

## broken fences

Last night I listened to Rachel share her story. Rachel is a beautiful single woman whom I have watched for years as she serves sacrificially and joyfully with children in our church. She's one of those people who just beams. You know. You see her and kind of want to hug her, even if you don't know her.

I sat for thirty minutes listening to her story, which I had never heard, shaking my head as tears fell and my mind raced. Rachel's life sounded more like the life of some character on *Grey's Anatomy* than a woman serving in our children's ministry. Her entire life she cared for herself while her parents fought and eventually divorced. As an only child, she fully depended on God—and she discovered earth-shattering things.

She told us that later, she found out her dad was not her biological father. Her biological dad was a married man, with another family, whom her mom had slept with, and Rachel still has never met him. He had written her letters during her childhood that she never got to read. They were kept from her and eventually thrown away. She has two half brothers whom she can never know without ruining their lives and family.

The parents who raised her went on to divorce, and the dad she'd always known remarried. His new wife began running up credit card debt in her name using her social security number. Rachel, who beams to the point of garnering spontaneous hugs, is the same woman being sued in court right now by creditors because the people who were supposed to love her and take care of her have betrayed her. As a single woman, she has had to handle this by herself until recently, when our church family came to her defense.

As she shared the story with us last night, Rachel was headed to spend Christmas with her family, those people who are the cause of her suffering. And so she asked for prayer. She prayed that she could show them Christ through this. How could she not feel like a victim?

Then she said a line I will never forget: "You have to thank God for the seemingly good and the seemingly bad because really, you don't know the difference." The hardest things in her life have brought her the deepest relationships. The hardest things have become the things that define the most beautiful things about her. The hardest things in her life have given her more of God.

Growing up, when I would try to pray and trust God with everything, pictures of the life I desperately wanted would flash before my eyes. The pictures seemed possible. They weren't bad dreams—certainly not evil. They could even be considered good. I was going to keep building the good life I had been building, and it seemed to be working. Because it was working for me, I thought it was working for God too. I appeared to be a good Christian. Isn't that what he wanted? It was safe and known and comfortable, and everyone looking in saw a family, a girl who loved God. Wasn't that enough?

I wanted it to be . . . and I think I genuinely thought it was enough.

Somewhere along the way, even with grace sung all around me, God had become morality to me. God had become the American dream. God had become a white Republican, and he wanted me to have a nice home and a nice family with a fence to keep us all safe.

Through all of Scripture, we see that people have always done this, defined God on their own terms. Tried to get around giving him complete control. Built their own lives. Adam and Eve wanted more power, so they didn't trust God; they trusted themselves. And all that followed is the same mess that follows us as we ignore the most obvious fact: God builds our lives whether we give him permission or not.

It is the fight for control that has us all tied up, while it's really an illusion anyway. We control because we are afraid of what may happen if we let go. Do we really think we are better captains of our lives than a God who sees everything and deeply loves us? So we pursue our scrapbook dreams, distracted, too busy to see he's already with us and has our steps planned. The days and pictures and people he puts in our scrapbooks are seemingly chaotic but perfectly planned.

> God builds our lives whether we give him permission or not.

The desire of God's heart is to deal with suffering—and it is not just his desire; it is his plan. Once he deals with it, it is over. He is patient in his judgment, desiring that none be lost (2 Peter 3:9).

If we believe the Bible, we must believe that the heart of our unpredictable, sovereign God is good, that he sees us and is for us, even though he allows this pain. As my friend Rachel discovered, who is to say what is good or bad anymore? Not till heaven will we know. From his eternal perspective, it's tolerable to allow our temporary dreams to fall apart. But we seize more of God when he seizes us through our broken dreams. He is wildly unpredictable, and learning to question and accept his ways is part of the journey of following an unsafe, invisible God. He calls the shots on what happens to us in this short stint here. He calls them, whether we want to let him or not. Our faith must remain greater than our pain and our fears.

We need different eyes, a different mind. One that lifts us above the seen and our short time here, above the fears that invade our lives, above the snapshots in our scrapbooks.

Do I trust God? Today as I write, I am in Colorado with my sister, Brooke, who just bravely delivered her daughter, little Lucy, twenty weeks too soon. Lucy is with Jesus. Today Brooke said through tears, "I trust God." The beauty of the statement on this day makes me cry. God, give us enough faith for whatever the stories of our lives will hold, even on the worst of days.

# eighty years

## abandoning this life

He wore little spectacles, just the type you would expect a pensive counselor to wear as he looked down his nose at you. His posture and stare made me nervously aware that he did not know exactly what to do with me.

I was there that day because I was a wreck. I was disillusioned and hurting from several years of a failing life. It felt all broken. I was there trying to be fixed. Zac and I had been married only a few years and could not land on peaceful territory. We had left our cozy lives, gone to seminary, and Zac had taken a job as a youth pastor in a small church. Ministry was no longer pats on the back and grateful thank-you notes. We were disappointing people in our church, and they weren't afraid to tell us how we were not measuring up to their expectations. We had stepped out and followed God. So why was my life spinning out of control?

I went into that counseling session so jaded. Things had been hard long enough to make me wonder if they would ever be okay again. I was all tied up inside, and I just couldn't tell how to let God help me. I still knew he was real, but I couldn't figure out how to untangle the inside of me. I remember sitting in that office, thinking, *Why would I continue giving my life to God if this is how hard it will always be?*

As if God owed me for serving him.

Theologian Tim Keller says if you love anything more than God, even though you believe in God, if there is anything in your life that is more important to your own identity or significance than God, then that is a false god and it is a power in your life.[5]

And you can usually tell that something here has become an idol because you have an extreme reaction when it is threatened.

Everything in my life was being threatened, and I was reacting extremely.

See, I was free for eternity and physically free, but I kept going back to the things I loved more than God. Keller says, "Old masters come back and tell you that you will die—you need me—you can't live without me. In one sense you are free but in another sense they come back and wave their finger at you."[6]

So we live more afraid of losing what we love here than of facing God in eternity, even when it all is striving after the wind, to paraphrase Solomon (Eccl. 1:14).

## far heavens

I was teaching a roomful of college girls at the University of Texas, beautiful young girls who were smart and had every opportunity and blessing this world offers. Yet every one of them held hurts, whether it was a daddy who had disappeared, a boy who had taken advantage, or a friend who had cut them out. So, though they possessed everything in the world, they sat waiting each week to see God. I did my best to make God big as I taught his Word, to give them hope because of Jesus and his plan for making it all right, to remind them that in a minute we would all be in heaven.

We had a lot of honest conversations about how all these God things are pertinent to the pain of being excluded or abandoned or shamed. In the midst of one of those nights, a girl raised her hand and made one of the simplest and yet most influential statements I've heard. I think it's something we've all thought at some point: "Heaven just feels so far away."

I sighed, thinking how quickly we would all be eighty years old and at the end of our lives.

A few minutes later, I got a call from my mom, but I ignored it since I was with the girls. When I got in the car and called her back, she told me my grandmom had just gone home to Jesus. All of a sudden I could taste heaven. It felt so far away when we thought about it moments before. But my grandmom, with whom I had so recently shared a meal, was instantly there. If we can taste heaven, we live differently.

Not that long ago, I was eight years old. I had on pink culottes and a white T-shirt with blue and green hearts on it. I was lying on the couch in my dad's study, looking up at the popcorn ceiling in very deep thought, and nothing in that moment was spectacular. This is a boring story because nothing happened that day. But I remember it perfectly because I seared it into my memory. I worked especially hard searing it for one reason. I lay there in my culottes, realizing what most people don't until they are in midlife. My life was going too fast. I thought, at eight years old, I was growing up too fast. I was a weird little kid.

Now, as I type this a few decades later, I have kids older than I was in that moment. In what felt like only a few years after I was eight, I was in my mid-twenties with a newborn baby boy. And a few years from now I will be sending them off to college. You get it. It goes fast.

## struggling waiting

A friend of mine spent the week at the beach recently, and her family got to observe sea turtles being born. She came home talking about them. The story reminded me of the day on the sofa while I sat puzzling about life with the counselor and his spectacles.

When a sea turtle is pregnant it crawls out of the sea and spends hours digging a hole in the sand in which to lay her fifty to two hundred eggs. Then she takes off, back to the ocean. After a few weeks, the babies hatch. They are born in a hole in the sand, with no mama, not knowing where they are and surrounded by others who don't know anything either. I would imagine they feel a little disoriented.

But they must know that that hole is not their home. It's uncomfortable, crowded, and dark. It really doesn't work for them at all. They instinctively start to crawl out of this place where they don't belong. Crawling is hard in the sand, with everyone pushing each other. Their tiny bodies have to go over seemingly huge barriers and past stragglers, as fast as possible because there are a million creatures out there that might eat them. I'm sure it feels like an eternity. *When am I going to be there?* they think in their tiny turtle brains. *How long is it going to take? Why am I here all alone? Where is it again that we are even going?* But they keep moving, straining forward, crawling toward what they believe they were created for. But what *were* they created for? If they are not made to stay in the sand, then how do they know what home is like?

What if they just stayed, decided that it was all just a myth— that great watery deep? After all, no other turtle they've met has

66

ever seen it. What if they decided it was just going to be too hard? Or what if, instead of following the voice we know to be God's telling them to move toward the water, they followed a crowd of confused turtles moving toward the lights of a hotel or highway? If they do not follow the voice inside them, they will miss the world they were truly created for, the joy that God has in store for them there. The ocean.

> If they do not follow the voice inside them, they will miss the world they were truly created for, the joy that God has in store for them there.

There is something about counseling offices and fights and sadness and fear that does not feel like home. It feels difficult and sandy, and we feel a little stuck, a little cramped.

## numbing flowers

One of the pastors who poured deeply into Zac and me, Tommy Nelson, gives a talk about the devil, called "If I Were the Devil." In his deep and dramatic Tom voice, he says,

> If I was the devil, I'd tell you what I'd do. I would try to deceive you and get you into error. I would get you off base. And if you still stayed true, I would try to disqualify you. I would get you immoral, I would get you where no one would believe what came out of your mouth. I would make you a tabloid, where nobody would believe you. I would remove your confidence until you were afraid to speak because your life was such a shamble. I would get you into sin. I would prowl like a roaring lion to devour you morally.
>
> And if I couldn't do that, I would try to make you successful. And I would distract you if I couldn't disqualify you. I would get you busy. I would get you so distracted to the gospel that no longer would your prayers be about holiness and souls. They would only

be about the bottom line in your business. I would get you materialistic, and no longer concerned about the spiritual nature of life. If I couldn't do that, I would divide you. If I couldn't divide you, I've almost lost you. You know what I'd do then? I'd discourage you. And then if I couldn't discourage you, I'd try death. I would try my best to kill you. That's what I would do to take you out.[7]

This reminds me of a story from one of the Percy Jackson books by Rick Riordan. In the first book, Percy and his friends have a clear mission to save his mother from the Greek god Hades. (I know, my kids may be pagans now.) One of their missions is to retrieve a tool they need from a casino in Las Vegas. As they walk through the casino, the people there offer them flowers that taste great, and they take them. But these flowers also numb them and cause them to lose track of time. Percy wakes up and realizes this before it is too late, when he meets a man who still thinks it is 1975. Percy immediately pushes away the flowers and grabs his oblivious friends, yelling at them, "Stop eating the flowers! Wake up!!"[8]

They were in noble pursuit of rescuing Percy's mother, and yet they got distracted, caught up in a numbness-induced, carefree party. They were wasting time.

In Luke 14 Jesus had a large crowd following him. I am sure he was thinking something like, *You are following me now because it is easy, but you do not know that following me may cost your lives.* And so he started talking about the cost of following him. He began with family, saying, "If anyone comes to me and does not hate his own father and mother and wife and children and brothers and sisters . . . he cannot be my disciple." And he moved even closer to home: unless you hate "even [your] own life, [you] cannot be my disciple."

We know from Jesus' strong commands to love even our enemies that he is not advocating neglecting our relationships or those who depend on us (Luke 6:27). He is saying,

*Wake up! This pursuit of me, it may cost you everything you hold dear, everything you love here. It may cost even your life. And until this life gets small, really small, and I get big, really big, you won't truly follow me. Because loving this life too much will affect your love for me. It also will affect what you are willing to do for me.*

Many of those standing listening to him went back to their lives. And a few of those who continued to follow him ended up being killed for Christ's name just a few years later.

He is ridiculously radical, our God. He is serious about us not loving anything more than we love him. I see it when I look at Abraham. He was willing to do *anything* for God.

Abraham adored God so much he was willing to leave everything he knew and follow him out into the wilderness. He had so much faith that God was real. He knew it, and he spent his life chasing after him. In Genesis 17 God promised Abraham a son who would father many nations and be the hope of the world. Abraham longed for God to deliver on this promise, even though his wife, Sarah, was infertile and could not have children. As they continued to age past the years of childbearing, Abraham began to question God. But finally, in their extreme old age, God miraculously blessed them with a son, and they called him Isaac.

*Until this life gets small, really small, and I get big, really big, you won't truly follow me.*

I adore my kids. If they are at camp or with grandparents for too long, I will physically ache to see them. When they were babies and looked like they were choking, my blood would rush and I would prepare to save their lives using the Heimlich maneuver, even though they were never really choking. But I would do anything to protect them and keep them close to me.

Abraham had waited his entire life for his boy, and no doubt he was in love with Isaac. But for the first time, God saw his man's loyalty shift. No longer was God Abraham's first love. Now Isaac had his heart, and Abraham's child came first.

So God did something terrifying and gruesome. He asked Abraham to sacrifice and kill his only beloved son. This is insane. Those of us who have heard this too many times need to stop and consider that this is the passionate and jealous nature of our God. Life is short to him, and eternity and having the God of the universe in the right place in our lives is more precious than our brief lives here.

Facing every parent's worst nightmare, Abraham took his son and his weapon, and they began the climb to the altar. Even though God didn't actually take Isaac's life in the end, Abraham was willing to give him up.

This is a sacrifice we will never face. But really, we do face something like it. Every day little gods compete for our primary affections. But when would anyone ever question a loving parent's adoration of his kids? This is surely not wrong! Yet God clearly says first and foremost, "Have no other gods before me" (Ex. 20:3). *Nothing here shall compare to me in your heart. Everything should so pale in comparison to me that it is as if you hated it.*

> Every day little gods compete for our primary affections . . . Yet God clearly says first and foremost, "Have no other gods before me" (Ex. 20:3).

With our minutes and days and decades, we build houses and savings accounts and busy calendars full of activity. And in some deeper way, we build our reputations and friendships and invest in our kids and careers. We are looking for this life to matter. No, we are actually looking for ourselves to matter. So we keep so busy, so distracted, so in love with everything but our invisible, patient, jealous God.

Christ said, "So therefore, any one of you who does not renounce all that he has cannot be my disciple" (Luke 14:33). This covers literally everything.

In essence, "Stop eating the flowers! Wake up!"

◦ ◦
◦ ◦

My friend David is a surgeon. Recently he came home and told his wife, Karisa, he was feeling led to move their family to a rural part of Ethiopia and open a health clinic. Obviously, Karisa was a little worried. Rural Ethiopia felt unsafe to her; she pictured her four young kids being raised without fences and locks and in an unfamiliar world.

David kindly asked her, "What are you most afraid of?"

Karisa said, "What if we die?"

David, with his intense eyes set on heaven, said in return, "Then what a way to die."

As I stand back and look at myself as I was, sitting in the counselor's office whining and crying after years of chasing things that were supposed to work for me, that were supposed to make me happy here, that God was supposed to do, I see that my ache was actually his mercy showing me that everything I loved other than him was never going to work. It was never supposed to work.

We love our earth. We love our people. We love our stuff. We love our schedules. We love our short lives here. And God is saying, *Look up. This is going fast. Your life here is barely a breath. There is more, way more.*

Time is almost gone. Our lives are only spent well on him and whatever stories he has written for us. What are we really so afraid of losing?

Heaven feels far away, and we forget. But it is real . . . and it is coming.

# PART 2

::

# praying anything

:: 8

# crashing curtains
## waking up

Zac and I were meeting several friends downtown at a nice Italian restaurant. The atmosphere was cozy and dark, almost leading us into deep, drawn-out conversations. That morning I had started my blog, written my first entry. I was not sure exactly why I was even writing. But that night God would begin to change our lives so drastically that I almost can't believe that was the day he had me start writing. It's as if it were to document the new life we were about to begin.

As with all uniform dinner conversations, we moved from the weather to kids to the interesting events and people we had recently encountered. One friend told a story about a young woman with whom she was connected in Uganda. Nothing about that moment hinted that my life was about to change, that God would use this story, this woman, to obliterate my current comfortable existence.

She told me the young woman, Katie Davis, was twenty-one. Katie grew up in one of the wealthiest parts of Nashville and visited Uganda with her mom when she was a junior in high school. She went on to graduate high school at the top of her class, sporting a yellow convertible and cute boyfriend, and had the capacity to go anywhere to college. But Katie, against her parents' desires, felt called to go back to Uganda for a year before college.

In that year God moved her heart to a place where she could not go back and carry on the normal life of a college student. She tried, but she was miserable. She knew God was calling her to Uganda, and this time for good. She left everything. Today Katie lives in Uganda with thirteen young girls whom she has adopted off the streets. As my friend went on describing this girl's life, my heart started beating out of my chest. My head spun with so many questions . . .

> I was still limiting God by my understanding of how life should work—safe and comfy and not so costly.

"Does she have help?"
"What do her parents think?"
"Isn't she too young?"
"Doesn't she need community?"
"Is she safe?"
"Doesn't she want to get married?"

These questions reveal how far I was from the place where I'd do anything for God. I was still limiting God by my understanding of how life should work—safe and comfy and not so costly. I don't remember anything else about that dinner from that point on . . . I don't know what I ate or what else was said. My mind was transfixed with this twentysomething, and I was just counting the moments until I could get home and pull up her blog.

We got home late, and I grabbed my computer. Zac was tired and headed to bed, so I sat on the bathroom floor in the dark and started reading. I read and read and read late into the night.

I read things like this:

All my life, I had everything this world says is important. In high
school I was class president, homecoming queen, top of my class. I
dated cute boys and drove a cute car. I had supportive parents who so
desired my success that they would pay for me to go to college anywhere my heart desired. BUT, I loved Jesus. Jesus says to Nicodemus
that in order to enter the Kingdom of Heaven, one must be born
again. Check. Jesus says to another guy that in order to enter the
Kingdom of Heaven one must sell everything they have and give it to
the poor and then COME, follow Him. Oh . . . I realized that I had
loved and admired and worshipped Jesus without doing what He did.
So I quit my life. Originally it was to be temporary, just a year before
I went back to normal Brentwood life and college. It wasn't possible.
I had seen what life was about and I couldn't pretend I didn't know.
So I quit my life again, but for good this time. I quit college, I quit my
cute designer jeans and my little yellow convertible. I quit my boyfriend. I no longer have everything that the world says is important.
BUT, I have everything that I know is important. I have never been
happier, and I have never been closer to the Lover of my Soul and my
Savior. JESUS wrecked my life, shattered it to put it back together
more beautifully. I am in LOVE with Him. Period.[1]

Now I was wrecked. At some point I started crying, hard. My
heart was broken. Every god I had built and stroked and justified fell
onto the bathroom floor that night with my tears. The life I was building was crashing before me. I grieved. I grieved the moment on my
parents' bed when I had cared more about their opinion than God's
quiet voice in me. I grieved the curtains I had pined for. I grieved the
control I had given to everyone around me by caring so much about
their opinions of me. I grieved the life I had built around a plastic god
and a pretend heaven that had only seemed slightly possible. I grieved

a life that was spent on myself, the excess I had justified while others suffered. I grieved sitting back and controlling my image rather than pouring out my life and gifts for his name's sake. I grieved that my mind had been spent solving my own simple problems rather than giving my life away for the few years I am here.

And then I saw God—the real God—and I saw the moment I would meet him. He was on his throne with eyes fixed on me, questioning why I had sought my comfort more than him. Why had I loved people more than him? Why had I sat on every gift he had given me to make him known? Because I cared more about being judged by everyone else but him?

> Why had I loved people more than him? Why had I sat on every gift he had given me to make him known? Because I cared more about being judged by everyone else but him?

I weep now again as I write this. I weep because I almost got away with a wasted life. What if I had blown off the interruptions he was offering? I might be stuck with the mediocre life I was so afraid of losing at the time. But it was like he lifted my head, while I was in a puddle on the bathroom floor, and let me see into his heart, into heaven, into the brokenness of those suffering, into my own soul. And in a moment what had never occurred to me made perfect sense. So much sense that I was willing . . . desperately willing . . . to do *anything*.

## lovely drinks with umbrellas

That night on the floor I told him, "From this point on things are changing. I am living for the moment when I will face you. I want to get to heaven out of breath, having willingly done anything that you—God of the universe—ask . . . anything."

Katie was a teenage girl in a remote African village who left her scrapbook and is now actually choosing suffering because she adores Jesus. He alone changed everything.

Her normal has been thrown out the window.

People are in their proper place and God is in his.

She is totally abandoned. Totally surrendered.

Problems are fading away.

This life is lost. The next is in full focus.

God seems real because she can see him from the edge.

God is alive, her best friend, her everything.

I remember being a new God-lover in high school, looking around at all the Christians I knew, and thinking, *Is everybody in denial? God is real and we are about to be in heaven! That should change everything!* And then at seminary, again, as I learned more about God, I looked around at the people who were hearing the same things I was, about heaven and hell and spiritual wars and forever, and I wanted to shake them because everyone was so calm about it. As though we were talking about whether to go see a movie or go out to eat.

And then, finally, I read the words of a human girl, and they resonated with me.

Maybe the best way to describe how I felt that night reading Katie's blog is to say that it felt as if I had been laying out, drinking something fruity with an umbrella in it on some beautiful cruise ship moving across the ocean. When I looked around, all the other people were having a nice time by the pool or walking on the deck with their friends.

"From this point on things are changing. I am living for the moment when I will face you. I want to get to heaven out of breath, having willingly done anything that you—God of the universe—ask . . . anything."

anything

But in the course of our beautiful day, the captain came over the loudspeaker, panicking, yelling to everyone, "This ship is sinking! Head for the rescue boats!" All the days in seminary classes, the night in front of the crosses, every time God and forever had tasted so real—felt like this.

So naturally I threw down my drink and started running for the boats, but quickly realized I was the only one. Everyone else seemed oblivious, just continuing their lovely vacation. It didn't sit well with me, but I didn't know what to do . . . I looked around, and everything did look rather pleasant and safe. So I went back to my drink and magazine thinking maybe I had imagined it.

But this feeling stayed in my gut: *Something is not right . . . I think this ship is going down, and everyone's losing it, because they are just sitting here acting lovely.* But I kept sipping my drink with an umbrella in it, lest they all think I'd gone crazy, running for the rescue boats on a perfectly lovely day. The captain's deep, pleading voice came over the speaker occasionally, and everybody remained unchanged. So I pushed away the pending reality and went back to being composed.

And then I saw Katie . . .

It was like seeing some fellow shipmate on the other side of the boat out of the corner of my eye, waving her arms with abandon, pointing to the rescue boats, doing everything she could to grab everybody and get them in with her. And in one moment, just from glimpsing her, the enormous reality that I sensed was confirmed: the captain's voice had been accurate. Ridiculous or not, that night after reading Katie's blog, my vacation was over and I was embracing what I knew to be true: the absurd reality that the ship

My vacation was over and I was embracing what I knew to be true: the absurd reality that the ship was going down and everyone was drinking drinks with umbrellas in them.

was going down and everyone was drinking drinks with umbrellas in them.

I had a constant, nagging feeling that God was real and this life wasn't a game; it wasn't about my comfort or my curtains or how much everyone liked me and approved of me. Heaven was coming, God's voice was clear, and I needed to quit pretending everything was lovely.

At another point I read this from Katie's blog:

Someone asked me the other day, "Really? Is it really as great as you make it sound? I could never do that! Are you really happy?"

For all of you who wonder, this is my response.

You know what I want sometimes? To go to the mall and spend a ridiculous amount of money on a cute new pair of shoes. I want to sit on my kitchen counter chatting with my girlfriends and eat a whole carton of cookie dough ice cream. I want to watch *Grey's Anatomy*, or any TV for that matter. I want to cuddle with my sweet boyfriend. I want to hop in my cute car, go to the grocery store, and pick up any kind of produce I want. I want to wake up in a house with my loving family, not all by myself. I want to go to Blockbuster and pick out a movie to watch with my little brother and his friends and I want to cook for them at midnight. I want to spend mindless hours with my best friends talking about boys and fashion and school and life. I want to go to the gym. I want my hair to look nice. I want to wear cut-off jean shorts. I want to be a normal teenager living in America. I do.

But.

You know what I want more? ALL the time? I want to be spiritually and emotionally filled every day of my life. I want to be loved and cuddled by 100 children and never go a day without laughing. I want to wake up to a rooster, my two Africa dogs, and a splendid view of the Nile river. I want to be challenged endlessly; I want to be learning and growing every minute. I want to be taught by those I teach. I want to share God's love with people who otherwise might not know it. I want to work so hard that I end every day filthy and too tired to move. I want to feel needed, important, used by the Lord. I want to make a difference and I want to follow the calling that God has planted deep in my heart. I want to give my life away, to serve the Lord with each breath, each second. I want to be here. Right here.[2]

After one night on a bathroom floor with God and my laptop, I was ready for bigger, better dreams. No longer was I composed, sipping drinks by the pool while people were dying. The highlights of my days had been similar to Katie's first desires: a great Starbucks first thing or watching *Wipe Out* with my kids or going out for Mexican food with friends . . . In one night God so shifted my reality that all I wanted was *more*. I was ready to run as hard as I could and join Katie in giving up earthly comfort to dramatically wave my arms and run for the rescue boats, dragging everyone I could . . . obeying the captain's voice.

# new eyes

## real change

After all dreams end, no matter the magical places they took you, the sun always comes up, you get out of bed, and you eat your breakfast and load the dishes. The morning after my dramatic bathroom-floor reckoning with God was no different. Normal pressed in. Real life was right where I'd left it prior to dinner the night before, pulling on me with its own set of demands and expectations.

Sometimes God feels more real than people. It's rare, but on occasion he moves and blows into a spot in some winsome, powerful way, and there is no denying he's there. After those rare, brief encounters, he is so real that you can feel him waiting for you. For a little while, before it wears off, you can close your eyes and picture heaven and hurt. And for a little while, before it wears off, if he asked you to, you would saw off your arm.

But then it fades. You know in your mind that he is still that real, but in your gut and your soul you forget and get numb.

I knew this was spiritual protocol. In my life up until that moment, God had shown up several times, and I knew this drill. In the past, those moments played a role in shaping me, building my story. But that morning while I was loading the dishes, I realized that this one felt different. It was the moment I had discovered C. S. Lewis's wardrobe and pushed through the fur coats. No longer would playing tag in the house to pass the time satisfy me when there was a land to explore, full of talking animals and war. I had seen another reality. But the laundry still had to be put away. And what else was I going to do? I couldn't just hop on the next plane to Africa . . . and was it even Africa? I didn't know what to do, so I just prayed and I finished the dishes.

I knew that when the breath of God had dripped off of me, I was not going back. I sensed in my gut that it wasn't an encounter that would shape my life: it was *the* encounter with God that would define my life. It was the moment I woke up.

## contracts with God

When I was in college, I had the privilege of meeting Bill Bright, the founder of Campus Crusade for Christ. Dr. Bright was so regular. So humble. He was not a tall or particularly handsome man. But I knew I was speaking with a man possessed by God. At the time he was doing his yearly fast of forty days. He sought to align his life completely with God's will. He was a man sure of God and heaven.

But it was not always this way. Before Dr. Bright died he gave an interview, even with tubes supplying his oxygen. He was about to go meet God. He talked about how when he was young, before knowing God, he was ambitious for this life. He and his wife, Vonette, had dreams of living in Bel Air in a beautiful home and building a successful business in Hollywood. Then one day God led him to a church in Hollywood where he was introduced to Christ.

After two years of marriage the Lord called Bill and Vonette to give him everything. They were willing to surrender their entire lives and do *anything*. Being a businessman, Bill wrote out and signed a contract with God signing over their lives, their future, their money, everything they had in 1951.

Twenty-four hours later God met with him and gave him a vision to reach the world: Campus Crusade for Christ. Bill said in the interview before he died, "Had there been no contract, in my opinion, there would have been no vision. God brought us to the place where we made total, absolute, irrevocable surrender. Then He knew He could trust us."[3]

Until there is total surrender, there is no vision.

Campus Crusade has gone on to reach people in more than 190 countries, with 27,000 trained staff worldwide. In its 57 years of ministry, Campus Crusade (now Cru) and its partnering ministries have exposed more than 8 billion people around the world to the gospel.

On July 19, 2003, Bill Bright went home to be with the Lord. On that day, some 8,000 Campus Crusade staff members and volunteers sat together in Colorado State's Moby gym at the biannual national staff conference. When staff received word of Bill's passing, a time of worship and celebration ensued. The conference emcee asked people to stand if they came to Christ as a result of Bill Bright personally sharing the gospel with them. With tears of joy and gladness, many in the gym rose to their feet. The sound of rejoicing in the gym that day was deafening.

**Until there is total surrender, there is no vision.**

Dr. Bright laid down this life, and in laying it down, God used him to guide thousands of lives into eternity. Was I willing to do the same?

The morning after, it didn't take long to remember what I had always known to be true: surrender is usually dying to self on a daily basis and most often found in the mundane. Lunches had to be made, conflict with some friends had to be resolved, and toilets still needed scrubbing.

I married the guy who drove eleven hours to take a girl on a second date . . . a girl who did not want to be normal. Zac is a church planter, and like many God followers, his life isn't complicated. If God is real, then you live like it. You read Scripture and obey it. Zac isn't emotional like me or prone to dramatic bathroom-floor encounters with God, but he gets God on a soul level and pragmatically, almost systematically, cuts up his life and disperses it out accordingly.

So when his wife confides she has been numb and apathetic and she wants to live differently, maybe sell the house, adopt, go to Africa, give away all the money . . .

He looks at her, at me, and says, "Okay."

I know that is not everyone's reality.

Maybe your husband doesn't even know God. Or perhaps, if you are single, your parents or friends would never understand taking risk for a God who may not seem real.

Surrender may include unconditionally respecting a spouse or family member who is not displaying the form of godliness you crave. This is such a sensitive subject because, as women, our obligations to our husbands and families often make us feel as though our lives are even more out of our control. But part of trusting this God and part of obeying him is participating in his plan for our relationships. For married women, running ahead of our husbands shows them we don't need them, shows them they can't lead us, that we are faster, deeper, and love God more. If you're married, know that making our husbands feel inferior is not God's will.

Zac and I had paid a price to have moments of unison like that. Years of counseling and fights made me wonder if God had made a mistake putting two strong-willed leaders like us together. But all of that was building something, making us one, even though at the time it felt as if parts of us were dying. In reality, they *were* dying—and that was okay; that was the plan.

I know that being unified in surrender to God may not be your reality, but God controls the hearts of kings and the hearts of our spouses and loved ones. He says things like this over and over again: "By this all people will know that you are my disciples, if you have love for one another" (John 13:35).

So if God is moving in you and calling you to surrender, but your loved ones are not there, love them and wait on God. Obey God. If you're married, be careful not to create a grand plan that God and your husband aren't a part of.

Through our love, we display our God, especially to our spouses and those closest to us. And through our radical submission to them, God moves.

## contagious

My husband, in his own beautiful and very different way, was in the same place . . . ready for more, ready for *anything*.

He dove into Katie's blog in the same addicted fashion that I had, and shortly after that time he gave an Easter sermon I will never forget. It was taken from 1 Corinthians 15. Paul says that because of what Jesus did and because of who I am in him, "if Christ has not been raised . . . 'Let us eat and drink, for tomorrow we die'" (vv. 17, 32).

But if Christ *has* been raised from the dead, *risk it all*.

For believers in an eternal God, it shouldn't be unusual to risk our entire lives for him. It should be the norm for every person who claims Christ.

It was all resonating with Zac too. One of two things was true. Either God is not real and everything will go black when we die, and we should live it up! Why are we all sitting around behaving ourselves if the only thing in the universe bigger than us is nothingness? *Or* God is real and he really sent his son in the form of a man to bleed out on assembled pieces of wood, to be the only worthy sacrifice, buying us from our sin, winning us back when we were running from him. And then he came back to life, because he was God. It's easy for us to take the resurrection for granted. But if you saw a man die and then three days later he was walking and eating and talking and appearing out of thin air, that would be a life-altering thing. He showed he was God. This is what we believe about Jesus.

> For believers in an eternal God, it shouldn't be unusual to risk our entire lives for him. It should be the norm for every person who claims Christ.

That should wreck everything else about our reality. And frantically wrecked people, they wave their arms a little—they are single-minded to the point of being considered absurd by those looking in. People like that do things . . . crazy things that mean something, since there *is* more to life than nothingness, and there is something bigger than us and our little story playing out on this spinning planet.

Zac's sermon was one that either made you so uncomfortable that you were dying for him to finish or it so resonated that you hung on every word. For a lot of the people closest to us, it was the latter. I wrote this on my blog at some point in the weeks that followed that sermon:

*Revival*
April 20, 2009

Here we go—this is what's been taking place:

1. It is as if everything I have said I believe is all of a sudden and miraculously real to me . . . heaven, God in me, freedom from bondage, my purpose here.
2. And because it is real, I am living as if it is real.
3. And living that way costs me something—costs me everything.
4. So we start to consider our priorities and realize we value things like comfort and people's opinions and happiness.
5. Then God says to die and sell everything we own and hate this life.
6. And we say okay.
7. We start thinking things like, *Should we sell our new house? Or We have an empty bed—let's fill it with a child who needs a home* and *let's invite our neighbors to Easter dinner.*
8. And then the people around us start saying things like, "Don't do it for the wrong reasons"—like the love of adventure or for our own glory. And we say, "Ok, thanks for the heads-up."
9. Then we have people who are praying the same prayers and thinking the same thoughts, and something is happening—not a feeling or love of adventure or desire for glory but something within us that is from God, a call to more: to die—to live.
10. My heart is bleeding and I can't make it stop. So we are praying and willing and dreaming of living for heaven instead of the American dream, and it is changing everything. And I am strangely okay with that.[4]

We were both ready and willing, and so were a lot of people close to us, but now what? What would he have us do?

We knew that this was not about accomplishing some visually stunning display of martyrdom or philanthropy. This surrender was simply an agreement with the living, active God of the universe saying he could have us for *anything*. We were his, and only through his Spirit would we know what to do—and only through his Spirit could we do it. Again, the only thing we knew to do was pray.

So we prayed . . .

# big God

## praying *anything*

"God we will do anything. *Anything.*"

That night, after we prayed *anything*, as I was falling asleep, I looked into God's eyes and asked him, *What do you want me to do while I'm here?*

We weren't as scared as we should have been. We were just so tired of normal. We loved our simple, sane life, but now we wanted to find the kind of life you only find if you lose normal, simple, and sane. God was real and heaven was coming, and I wanted to hold every moment on earth in light of that moment when I would meet God face-to-face.

I was ready to forsake this life for the next. I wanted him to un-reservedly have me, so that when I faced him, we would both know

> I wanted to be right with God at the end of my life rather than right with all the people in it.

that my life was spent on everything he had dreamed for me. I wanted to be right with God at the end of my life rather than right with all the people in it.

The night we prayed *anything*, God was ready to have his way with us. Actually, he sits around waiting for that sort of thing. "For the eyes of the LORD run to and fro throughout the whole earth, to give strong support to those whose heart is blameless toward him" (2 Chron. 16:9).

## waking up

We are not the only passionate generation ready to forsake this life. Many have sold out before us, and their lives have marked history.

D. L. Moody was a poorly educated, unordained shoe salesman who felt God's call to preach the gospel. His bathroom-floor moment came early one morning when he and some friends gathered in a hay field for prayer and confession. His friend Henry Varley said to this young group of men, "The world has yet to see what God can do with and for and through and in a man who is fully and wholly consecrated to Him."[5]

Moody spent the rest of his life trying to be a man wholly given to God—willing to do anything. From that point on, Moody was a dead man walking, waving his arms, pleading because a different reality was coming. He was uneducated, armed with only the gospel, no agenda of his own, but completely abandoned to God. His short, passionate life affected heaven forever.

Through the course of Moody's life, tens of thousands found God or came back to faith. Schools began out of the ministry of an uneducated man. Moody founded the Moody Bible Institute, which earned a reputation as "the 'West Point' of Christian work."[6] It has gone on to disciple Christian leaders for generations.

"The world has yet to see what God can do with and for and through and in a man who is fully and wholly consecrated to Him." I don't know if the world has seen it yet, but I do think we've found ourselves in the midst of a generation who would like to try. I want to try.

I look around and see currents that have dug deep crevices in our culture and eventually carved into our souls. Currents that make us think,

- *This seventy to eighty years of a life feel long and important.*
- *Comfort and safety are worthy pursuits.*
- *Stuff matters.*
- *Happiness is my right as an American.*
- *Moral living pleases God.*

As a generation, I believe we are all yawning and waking up, identifying these currents, and comparing them to the truth of God. We're considering this simple but game-changing thought: *If God is really real and we are going to live with him forever, shouldn't he be the only thing? Shouldn't he be the controlling force of our lives? If we really believe this . . .*

As a generation, we feel a growing desire to keep from turning into the kinds of religious people God looked at while he was on earth, when he said, "This people draw near with their mouth and honor me with their lips, while their hearts are far from me" (Isa. 29:13).

## child faith

Not long after my older daughter put her faith in Christ, we were driving and talking about her best friends. Kate rattled off several names, being the socialite of the preschool that she was. My son interrupted her with a smart-aleck, six-year-old's response, "Kate, God is supposed to be your best friend."

Before I could knock him over the head, a little Kate wisely responded, "We just met. I am just getting to know him, Conner."

Kate knew she was on a journey that was just starting. She wasn't going to pretend she and God were closer than they actually were yet. She wasn't going to fake it.

Many of us are awake enough that we have stopped pretending. I like that about our generation. I think we are pretty black-and-white, and if we don't know for sure, we keep our mouths closed. Something is building—I see it spreading through the ship, from Katie Davis to authors like Francis Chan and David Platt, all waving their arms. More and more people are waking up. It is spreading.

And everyone is asking the question, *do I believe in the invisible enough that I'm willing to live for it?*

It is a call to childlike faith. The simple reaction a child has to truth is to believe, act, and live as if truth is true. Simply. Recklessly. Christ said: "Truly, I say to you, unless you turn and become like children, you will never enter the kingdom of heaven" (Matt. 18:3).

> Do I believe in the invisible enough that I'm willing to live for it?

When my son Conner was four, he was learning to take everything to God and believe that he is real, that God hears him and answers him. This was about the same time he was learning about snow, which he had never seen, since we're in Texas. So he stepped out in full surrender to God and he passionately prayed for weeks for God to let it snow.

As the weeks turned into months, spring came to Texas. I wanted to stop his prayers, believing there was just no way it would snow this late so far south. But this was the most sincerely I had ever heard him pray for anything. With childlike faith my son was betting all he had, pushing all his little chips in, directing all his faith and passion toward his God. He knew God was real—and he knew he was the one who held the keys to storehouses of snow.

The temperature was getting higher as spring pressed in, but then, completely unprecedented and out of the blue, Zac and I saw a remarkable report from the weather guy on the evening news. With as much disbelief as all who were listening, he told us it was going to snow the next day.

Sure enough, for one glorious day in March, my kids and all of the Dallas–Fort Worth metroplex (thanks to my son) made snowmen and threw snowballs all day. It was back up to seventy degrees a few days later.

God saw a simple, child's heart betting almost foolishly on his reality, and just because God could, he delivered some of his snow for my son. God rarely indulges these little requests and at times it can seem he is even holding out on the most important things. His ways are not like ours. He is mysterious and moves as he wills. But he wants us, like children, to keep an unreserved faith in him, simply because he is God.

> He wants us, like children, to keep an unreserved faith in him, simply because he is God.

## not foolish

Jim Elliot was a zealot. After graduating Wheaton College, with friends and family persuading him to take a youth ministry position in the States, he considered the American church "well-fed" and decided that international missions should take precedence. He believed God was real, and Jim wanted to spend this life in reckless abandon for God's causes. He and his wife, Elisabeth, along with several of their friends, ran to the places in the sinking ship that had never even heard the captain's voice. They wanted to reach a people group in Ecuador called the Waodani.

Jim and his friends knew these men would likely try to kill them; this was the Waodanis' reputation. They first stayed in Quito, studying Spanish, and then moved to the jungle. They settled at the Shandia mission station, where their only child, Valerie, was born in 1955.

Jim, four other missionaries, and their pilot made contact with the Waodanis from their airplane using a loudspeaker and a basket to pass down gifts. After several months, the men decided to build a base along the river a short distance from the village. There they were approached once by a small group of Waodani and even gave an airplane ride to one curious Waodani. Encouraged by these friendly encounters, they began plans to visit the village. However, when their plane landed on January 8, 1956, Waodoni warriors killed Jim and his four companions instantly. Elliot's body was found downstream, along with those of the other men.

Later this entry was found in his journal: "He is no fool who gives what he cannot keep to gain what he cannot lose."[7]

Some time later Elizabeth and the other wives went back to the tribe that had brutally killed their husbands. Because of the women's unconditional love and desperate forgiveness, many within the tribe accepted Christ and were eternally saved.

*Anything* is not foolish if you believe in heaven. What else can we do? If Christ is raised from the dead, we risk it all, losing what we cannot keep to gain what we cannot lose. That is not foolish. That is common sense.

These missionaries were very ordinary, but God used them in extraordinary ways simply because they were totally abandoned to him. If you look at every significant impact for God's kingdom—from Paul in Acts to D. L. Moody to Billy Graham to Mother Teresa to Katie in Uganda—these were all average people, sometimes the least likely people, who were just completely resigned to God.

Zac and I wanted in. We wanted into the stories that last forever. We wanted to quit chasing the wind and building this short life. We wanted to not just offer God words but truly offer up our lives and all that was in them, letting go of every expectation of what he would say.

"God, we will do anything. *Anything.*" Our lives now lay in the hands of a reckless, invisible God.

# a thousand problems

## God rushes in

We prayed *anything* every night for a week. Every night we offered up something else to God as though we were little kids; we lifted up our house to him as if it were a little red plastic Monopoly house that we were willing to trade him. We were desperate to hear from him. And the interesting and beautiful thing is, God got really loud. We could feel him leading us, yes or no. After twenty-four hours of offering him our house, we knew we weren't supposed to sell it yet.

That was the first thing we offered him because it was financially the most valuable thing we owned, and we had just spent six months building it. It wasn't just a house—it was the first place we had hung curtains and unpacked the china. In a matter of a few weeks, the thing that had captivated my heart for years was easy to lift up to God, and I was shockingly content with whatever he said. I felt little connection to this thing that had once completely mastered me. God had shifted everything, and I truly couldn't believe how joyful we felt while dreaming about what God could do with the money from our house. But for reasons I see now, it wasn't time for that yet, and God knew we were going to need a secure and stable place from which to navigate the things he wanted us to do next.

The second night we prayed *anything* again. That night I kept picturing the empty bed in my son's room. And so we prayed, "God, do you want us to use the empty bed?" Again, surprised at how loud and clear our invisible God was all of a sudden, Zac and I both knew without a doubt that he was saying yes. But should we adopt, foster, or host someone temporarily? *Who do you want to use it for?* We did not know yet.

In our game of Monopoly, God gave us the red plastic house back but took the bed. It was a matter of time before it would be filled, but the prospect of that scared me more than selling our house. Our family just fit. It worked. Our kids were flexible and similar to Zac and me—they were fun-loving and easy, and we fit together like a perfectly matched team. I could not imagine risking the comfy way we fit together for a wild card. But I pushed this feeling away, knowing good and well that these decisions were no longer up to me. No more pro-and-con lists. No more scrapbooks of my future. No more seemingly logical decisions about what made sense for a family. Wild was the new expectation for our lives because we had given them entirely to a wild God.

The following nights brought more and more offerings of the little pieces of our lives to which we had attached ourselves. We offered the church. Did God want Zac's gifts somewhere else, or our church in the hands of a different leader? We offered him America. We were willing to turn over the church and go overseas if that would be the best way for us to glorify him while we were still here. Again we felt him leading us—*not yet*.

God wanted some of the things we offered, and he sent some back to our pockets for our use with not so much as a nod. He did not reveal what he wanted us to do with all of it yet. He was just clearly showing us the pieces of our lives that he would like to use in the coming years. He was sorting through our Monopoly pieces and claiming all of them but selecting a few he wanted to cash in immediately.

## a thousand problems

Praying *anything* was just the beginning for us . . . it was the beginning of something reckless and unknown. I knew God would change our circumstances. I knew he would begin to divide us up and pour us out wherever he wanted.

But I did not realize the impact it would immediately have on my soul. So much of my life and mind had spent significant time in places such as fear and discontentment and shame. As we lay in bed letting go of pieces of our lives that had seemed to be so important, sins and strongholds began to fall off of us. God was changing me. Everything was changing.

A. W. Tozer once wrote that if we exalt God to his right place in our lives, "a thousand minor problems will be solved at once."[8]

Christ wrote it this way: "Seek first the kingdom of God and his righteousness, and all these things will be added to you" (Matt. 6:33).

Before praying, I had been living so stuck . . . so numb . . . so screwed up and broken. I had a thousand minor problems, and everyone I knew had them too. I wanted to be fixed and healed, and I read all the books and followed all the steps and quite honestly was more stuck and broken than before.

When my kids would talk back to me in public, I would overreact because I was embarrassed. Or when I would let someone down by being late, I would get stuck in an over-reactive feeling of shame. I was ridden with anxiety about the church and all the people I wanted to please. I often felt sad, and I couldn't even determine its cause.

These struggles and others like them were simply the evidence of a plastic god; I doubted God was alive and working and seeing me. These struggles were evidence of how much I loved this short life more than the next one that never ends. I was trying to measure up with my behavior, striving for perfection.

> If someone had told me these problems would shrink if I would just surrender everything to God, I would have written them off as a cliché.

I saw friends walking through broken marriages, and they were so full of anger. I saw other friends battling years of depression. Some of them weren't mad or depressed but simply numb and distracted, always discontent and seeking the next new thing.

If someone had told me these problems would shrink if I would just surrender everything to God, I would have written them off as a cliché . . . "Jesus is the answer." I wouldn't disagree; I just wouldn't be able to take such a statement and push it down into the broken places in my soul. Honestly, before, surrendering to God had felt like bondage rather than freedom, binding myself to him and his will on a daily basis no matter the cost.

So how do we actually let God change us?

Not long ago we were on the lake in Austin with some friends. We pulled the boat up about twenty yards from some cliffs. I told my two oldest they should climb up and jump off. They excitedly hopped off the boat into the water, swam over to the shore, and began climbing up to the cliffs. We were a little too far away to hear them, and they couldn't hear us unless we screamed. So I just watched as the two of them, brother and sister, sat together at the top of the cliff discussing whether or not they should jump. You could tell my oldest son was the most unsure just by his body language.

I sat a little helpless, hoping they could do it; there really wasn't another safe way down. I knew that feeling they were having—a combination of adrenaline and fear and nausea. The only way to get over that feeling is to jump or crawl down.

Jump or crawl down.

When we've got our lives in our gripped hands and we consider handing them over, most of us get that feeling—fear mixed with adrenaline mixed with nausea. It feels as though we might die if we jump. But when I prayed *anything*, what I feared would bind me set me free. It stung like death, and it still feels like death, but that feeling is the key turning in the lock. On the other side of the pain is freedom, peace, joy, hope, the loss of control, and it is how I was made to live.

My kids eventually jumped—and then they jumped and they jumped and they jumped. We finally had to pull them in before dark. What if they hadn't tried?

We press through the doubts and the fears and we trust because God is trustworthy, and he knows how life is best lived. The more we jump and see our God come alive around us, the more we jump without fear—and the bigger the cliffs get.

> The more we jump and see our God come alive around us, the more we jump without fear—and the bigger the cliffs get.

I love this verse in Romans 6: "One who has died [with Christ] has been set free from sin" (v. 7). Something about dying to this life, all our rights and expectations, frees us.

Christ made some backward statements while he was here—some statements I don't think I have ever really believed.

"Blessed are the poor in spirit" (Matt. 5:3).
"Blessed are those who mourn" (Matt. 5:4).
"Blessed are those who are persecuted" (Matt. 5:10).
"Blessed are you when others revile you and persecute you and utter all kinds of evil against you falsely on my account" (Matt. 5:11).
"Rejoice and be glad" (Matt. 5:12).

Why?

Because to suffer in this life, to sacrifice for the name of Christ, means your reward will be great in heaven. Suffering affects my life for eternity in a positive way. I've never lived that way. I've lived trying to fix everything hurting in me with counseling and a good latte.

And while none of that is bad, it never fully worked. I still hurt.

> Suffering affects my life for eternity in a positive way.

What I wasn't told is that it is supposed to hurt. War isn't supposed to feel easy and comfortable and happy.

Through all my years growing up in the church, I had managed to escape any callings that felt too radical. *Die. Abandon. Yield everything.* These were words reserved for emotional moments on retreats, maybe for missionaries, but not for every day of my life. To walk and live out the gospel, to pick up my cross daily and follow Christ, felt very radical and unfortunately costly.

I'd have to learn to bite my lip when I knew I was right in a fight with Zac. To pursue reconciliation with someone who had hurt me rather than let it fester. To let the person who just drove up have the parking space rather than fight her for it. To put away the hundredth load of laundry. Daily abandon would prove to be more costly than the reckless kinds of obedience. I leaned into God harder than I had been. When I leaned in, he helped. Picturing heaven helped too.

I didn't need to be right so bad when I thought about God watching. I wanted to forgive when I thought about Christ's astounding mercy and sacrifice. And I'd better take care of my laundry and other business if heaven is coming. I wanted time for the other things God was leading us toward. And somehow in all the little deaths, in seeing more of God, I was watching my soul untangle.

But I wasn't going to get out of the radical reckless stuff either.

## undivided heart

One of the clearest things God said to me and to Zac that week was that I needed to start using my gifts. I needed to start writing and teaching. It was not clear what that meant, but I knew this wasn't about me. I was to be the pawn here—not because I was special, only willing. Even though I felt a little sick at putting myself out there, I remembered Mary, mother of Christ, saying, "I am the servant of the Lord; let it be to me according to your word" (Luke 1:38).

Most of my life I was looking for God to lead me loud and clear as he had for Mary with the angel. I had listened to sermons and read books about how to know the will of God. And with one simple, sincere prayer, he came flooding out of the woodwork as though he had been just waiting for this all my life. In the days to come, as I processed this, God started clearly bringing to life Scriptures I had read a hundred times.

Through these Scriptures God was explaining to me,

> I was to be the pawn here—not because I was special, only willing.

anything

*Jennie, you hear me now so loudly and clearly because* . . .

"I am the LORD, that is My name;

my glory I give [or share] to no other." (Isa. 42:8)

*And that is what you have been asking me to do until now. To share my glory. And I knew, Jennie, that*

"no servant can serve two masters, for either he will hate the one and love the other, or he will be devoted to the one and despise the other." (Luke 16:13)

*So I was waiting. I was waiting to be the only thing. As with Martha, when I was in her living room while I was here in the flesh.*

*She was worried and upset about many things, but only one thing was needed. Mary had chosen the good portion, and it would not be taken away from her* (Luke 10:41–42).

*Mary had chosen me above every other thing—nothing was more important to her than me. Nothing mattered here but me.*

*When the rich man wanted me but wasn't willing to do anything, I had to show him he still loved something more, that he had another master, so I told him,*

"You lack one thing: go, sell all that you have and give to the poor, and you will have treasure in heaven; and come, follow me." (Mark 10:21)

*And he wouldn't. He left me. He chose this life. See, I don't compete.*

*I was waiting, Jennie, calling you. I was waiting for you to see that while you wanted me all of these years, you had another master. Your heart was divided. You loved something else more, and I will not share my glory. I had to become your one thing* . . . *your only thing.*

*And so now* . . . *you will be hearing from me a little more.*

# dominoes

## no turning back

Following that week of praying and hearing from God, we stopped praying *anything*. I think our heads were full, and honestly, we were a little freaked-out. God was speaking, and while the details were hazy, we were getting the general idea of what he was saying. And it wasn't small. It wasn't easy stuff.

Somewhere in my life I picked up the idea that if things did not feel right or fall perfectly into place, God was not in them. I thought obeying God should feel pretty easy and convenient. For instance, if God was calling you to Africa, then he would have a buyer for your house in two weeks; and if not, then he likely isn't in it. Okay, maybe not that extreme, but if obeying seemed too uncomfortable, I likely would have decided that it wasn't from God. Where did I get that?

In Scripture God promises we will have trouble in this world.

Christ says, *If you are for Me, then the world will be against you. If you are not willing to lose everything you have, including your life, don't even follow me. Expect persecution, and consider that a privilege* (Matt. 12:30, Luke 14:26, and Matt. 5:10, paraphrased).

> Somewhere in my life I picked up the idea that if things did not feel right or fall perfectly into place, God was not in them.

All my life I thought I had God's stamp of approval because my life wasn't going badly. Now I was faced with the fear that it might actually be the opposite. What if my life was going so beautifully because I wasn't chasing after God?

Even though the thousand problems in my soul had shifted toward one goal and one hope and I felt free, I had one new problem: life was getting hard, the pace was picking up, and I felt reluctant. I wrote this as I began this journey.

*Reluctance*
May 5, 2009

What if he actually told me what it is he wants me to do . . . and I don't want to do it?

We are in a vulnerable spot. We have told him we will do anything. Anything that he calls us to, we will do . . . anything.

Go. Stay. Speak. Be quiet. Stand up. Sit down. Redeem children. Redeem dirty dishes. Something big. Something small. Anything drastic. Nothing fancy. Anything.

That I may know him and the power of his resurrection, and may share his sufferings, becoming like him in his death, that by *any means possible* I may attain the resurrection from the dead. (Philippians 3:10–11, emphasis added)

I want to know Christ . . . Yes!

And the power of his resurrection . . . Yes!

And the fellowship of sharing in his suffering . . . um . . . maybe?

Becoming like him in his death . . . not at all!

Could I have Starbucks while I decide?

And somehow to attain to the resurrection of the dead . . . big YES!

Please, somehow, God save me!

Some days I am willing and some days I feel reluctant.

Maybe I could do whatever big or small things if he would help me . . .

God, overcome me. Please.

## superman

We were in. We signed on the line. There was no turning back, but the deeper we were falling into this rabbit hole of obedience, the more out of control our lives began to feel.

Can you even imagine the day after Mary heard from the angel that she was pregnant with the son of God? There are no categories for this; it was so supernatural. Her true belief in God was evidenced in the denial of herself and the consequences of obedience. The immediate consequences—potentially losing her fiancé and possibly all respect in her society—paled to Mary in light of her God and her calling. Before she even had a chance to process all this, she escaped to her cousin Elizabeth's house. And when she arrived, she started praising God in the most beautiful song:

*"My soul magnifies the Lord,*
   *and my spirit rejoices in God my Savior,*
      *for he has looked on the humble estate of his servant.*
*For behold, from now on all generations will call me blessed;*
   *for he who is mighty has done great things for me,*
      *and holy is his name.*

*And his mercy is for those who fear him*
*from generation to generation."* (Luke 1:46–50)

With no regard for the way this would impact her short life here, she looked for the big picture. She saw that this was going to save generations of humans. She felt the eternal significance of her life and praised God that she got to be part of his plan, part of his plan to redeem people. No matter the suffering she would have in this life, she was praising God for a chance to participate in eternity.

> No matter the suffering she would have in this life, she was praising God for a chance to participate in eternity.

This was around the time that I had gathered the group of women in my living room to study the life of Mary. These women were also in the midst of change and obedience. Our first time together, I remember not even having words for all that was swirling around me. I brought us together because I needed to journey with some friends through this dark but exciting time. I needed to study God's part in it with other women who also wanted to yield everything. And so we chose to study Mary, a woman who lived a beautiful life amid a weighty call and God-induced suffering.

Mary never sought her own comfort.

She lived entitled to nothing.

She expected suffering rather than being surprised by it.

She waited and responded to God rather than trying to control any outcome.

She submitted to her husband's leadership over and over again.

She received whatever the Lord had for her with joy.

I had prayed the prayer of *anything* as though I were about to launch on the Superman ride at Six Flags, my eyes closed tight and fingernails digging in. I was so afraid.

I can just imagine God thinking something like, *Thanks a lot, Jennie. Great. You'll be used by me, but no one else will want to ever be, because you are making it look so terrifying!*

But on the other hand maybe he was thinking, *I love that she realizes she is going to need me for this.*

I have; I do need him. That has been the theme of the last two years of my life, and I see no relief in the future. He has stretched me to the places where fear should be paralyzing me, and yet I am okay.

As I looked at Mary, I saw a girl who surely did not feel worthy or able to bear and raise the son of God, but she did not focus on that. She submitted and focused on the eternal plans of God, and when she did that, she was just in awe that she got to be part of them. The cost and her inadequacy paled in light of God's plan for humanity. She just was in awe that God would have plans for her simple, short life here.

I had prayed the prayer of *anything* as though I were about to launch on the Superman ride at Six Flags, my eyes closed tight and fingernails digging in.

In America, we've learned the art of being verbally passionate but highly unresponsive Christ followers. Christ says over and over again, there is no such thing. So we are inadequate. We had better feel that. On the edge, you always feel it.

My husband once made me ride the Six Flags Superman ride with him in Arlington. As I sat strapped in, I felt the stillness and I knew what was coming was going to be fantastically horrifying (really—people have actually died on this thing). But I couldn't help myself; we love to do fantastically horrifying things for some reason. And now it was too late. I was strapped in and couldn't get off. My heart raced and I thought I might throw up. Yet all I had to do was hold on and scream. The ride did the work. I just held on and screamed.

Many people I loved were running, risking, letting go, and most of us were scared to death. Most of the things God was asking us to do required faith and trust deeper than we had previously tasted. God did not seem too worried about what the people in Scripture thought about their callings; he handed them out even if they felt reluctant or unsure about their assignments. Moses and Jonah and Esther all wished their callings away. But in their obedience, God was changing the world and building his stories.

Soon, on top of his terrifyingly clear desire for me to write and speak, God told Zac and me conclusively that his story for us included bringing a new person into our family. The thought of adoption followed us everywhere. The bed in my son's room wouldn't be empty for long. Thinking of all the details and everything that could go wrong was more terrifying than the Superman ride ever could have been. I held on to God with white knuckles.

My friend Karen looked at me a few days ago and said, "I feel like when I see you, Jennie, I am watching Lucy in the movie *The Lion, the Witch and the Wardrobe* as she rides to battle on the back of Aslan. Aslan is running wild to battle, and she is clutching his fur, just trying to hold on for her life. When they arrive, everyone has been turned to stone. Aslan begins to turn them, miraculously turn them back to flesh. And Lucy, she gets to be part of that! She just held on for the wild ride and she gets to see all of that."

> Despite all my fear, I wanted to not miss a thing.

All Lucy did was hang on and believe. She believed. God wants all of us to be a part of these stories with him, and because she hung on, she participated in the most moving of stories, winning wars and healing and restoring souls. This is the epic stuff spiritual life is made of. I wanted to hold on. Despite all my fear, I wanted to not miss a thing.

I wrote this in midst of my struggle:

*Falling into Obedience*
September 28, 2010

Everyone is surprised by how heavy I have been lately. "Isn't it so exciting, what God has called you to do?" they ask.

But so many things about obeying him are weighty. I am afraid of my capacity to do all of this. I hate being out there for scrutiny. I am afraid of what some of it will mean for my family and so many other things.

So why do it?

What if these little acts of obedience were a small part of a matrix of dominoes unfolding the glory of God (small because, after all, I am a small domino in a huge matrix). Could he bypass me and find another route? Of course—he is God.

But what if I laid down my life, my domino, and through that unleashed an army of others who laid down and unleashed their obedience, and through this matrix, God's glory was displayed through the laying down of lives in the midst of a generation?

Just in case God has given me these ridiculous opportunities to display his glory, we (my husband and I) feel compelled to obey, no matter the cost and uncertainty.

Because heaven is coming . . . and soon none of us will care about any other glory but his anyway.

I have many dominoes that have fallen behind me to allow me to fall . . .

Watching friends fall into adoption prepared our hearts for falling into adoption.

And too many mentors and friends to mention today have fallen into my life to help me to fall into ministry through writing.

We are all dominoes in this . . . we all have our place in this. What is yours?

I beg you—all of us—to fall. Fall into obedience that will shape the glory of God in our generation. We don't want to get to heaven and realize we missed it, that God rerouted around us . . .

Besides, I have this feeling these things God has for us may be the best things in life. I don't want to miss them.[9]

I knew before the ride ever took off . . . all I needed to do was trust and let it happen.

# spreading insanity

## lots of yes

When you turn your life over to a living God who sees need, who loves desperately, the way he chooses to pour you out will be as unique as the way he formed you in the womb and placed you in your space on the earth. Some of our *anythings* feel flashy and fancy, but most of our *anythings* fall in secret places.

> Some of our *anythings* feel flashy and fancy, but most of our *anythings* fall in secret places.

We weren't alone. This was contagious. It felt as though everyone else was feeling the same as we were, wondering if there was more, wondering if that voice was real and if we all should consider our numb vacation over. And as more and more of us hopped up running, even more joined in. It was spreading. And the beautiful thing was, each person's *anything* was completely unique. God was leading each person the way he was leading us.

Laura, my friend who had been bold enough to embrace her crisis of faith, had finished her year of wrestling to find God. She realized that in all the years of her ministry she'd lived with huge misconceptions of who God really was, borrowing and building on everyone else's faith. And now the crane that had helped her as she teetered over the edge had taken her from emptiness and placed her in the arms of the living, true God. She was completely taken with Jesus, what he had done for her, and the patient, loving way he let her process and find him.

Soon after landing, Laura sat in church and listened as my husband described what we were learning about adoption. Zac spoke of the beauty of recognizing all that God did for us when he loved and adopted us, and in turn giving that away to others who need to be adopted physically. Laura and her husband were finished having kids. But Laura felt it fresh. God had lovingly adopted her, bought her back, even though she was trying to run from him. And all of the sudden he was so clear to her and her husband . . . speaking and leading them. She walked up to me after that service, saying, "God wants us to adopt now." Like it was no big deal. God, whom she wasn't even sure existed a year earlier, was busting up their comfortable lives— and she wasn't even blinking.

Laura is Caucasian and her husband is Asian. It seemed the obvious, easy fit to adopt an Asian baby in need of a home. But God began closing doors. I recently went to the airport to meet their beautiful Rwandan daughter. Their mixed family just got more beautiful.

## africa here

While Katie was in Africa shaking everyone up, God was starting to move closer to home.

Bekah and Brandon are some of our best friends. Years ago, while Bekah and I were just getting to know each other, I sensed she was a good, safe friend and also not afraid to put me in my place when I needed it. So one night while we were hanging out with all our kids running wild, I asked her to be my friend. She thought I was kidding; it was a first-grade kind of question. But I wanted to intentionally invite her into the deepest spaces of my life.

Brandon and Zac share a similar friendship. Bek and Brandon have three precious kids and live in the suburbs of Austin, where they have been loving and serving their neighbors and those Brandon worked with in construction. One coworker of Brandon's, Andrea, was going through a really difficult time; she didn't know Christ and didn't have any community to help her. So they were helping her get on her feet. They were also praying *anything*. Bekah wrote us this e-mail:

Subject: My Africa

Friends, I've been a tad envious of Katie in Uganda . . . and been trying to figure out how I (my whole family for that matter) can get over to Africa . . . to avoid the lies that I'm so caught up with here in America . . . but also so that I will freely express and share Christ with those who don't know Him!

Tonight I experienced Africa by forgetting about the junk that usually distracts me and taking Andrea to Starbucks and sharing Christ with her. She prayed to receive Christ tonight. God was and is at work in our own backyard! Andrea accepted Christ tonight and is now a child of God! Doubt I'll get any sleep . . . He is wrecking my life and I'm loving it . . . Loving Him!

Bekah

Christy and Brian began their journey of *anything* when they gave up their comforts near their family and moved to Austin to help start the church with us. Together we have seen God move around us; something about being on this mission together is unusually bonding. It's almost like we can read each other's minds now because we have been on so many battlefields together. Brian is an accountant, and Christy stays at home raising their two beautiful kids.

She wrote me this in an e-mail:

I think my journey to total abandonment started over a period of time. I think God brought me to my knees, mostly through tragedy. That's when I realized just "why" we were put on this earth. It wasn't to live for myself, to hold tightly to my family and friends, to give half of myself to Him . . . it was to give 100 percent of myself to Him 100 percent of the time no matter what the cost. Scary? Of course. But I have to believe that "I will see the goodness of the LORD in the land of the living! Wait for the LORD; be strong and take heart and wait for the LORD!" (Psalm 27:13–14).

What happened when I gave in to God? I felt freedom and purpose in my life for probably the first time. I was tired of living a life without purpose. I knew he made me for something. To pour our lives into discarded children who have been through hell and back. That is what he is calling us to do. And it's costly! And I have to die to self daily. Making a decision to be "totally abandoned" is not a one-time thing for me. I daily have to remind myself why I'm here on this earth. And there are days when I hourly have to remind myself.

Christy

Christy and Brian just said good-bye to their first foster child. It was one of the hardest things I've ever had to watch. Their kids cried, missing what felt like a sister. But Christy said, "If it didn't hurt this much, then we didn't do it right." They are choosing pain.

*Anything* was playing out around us. This was about the same time the country was feeling the effects of the economic downturn. A lot of people in our church were suddenly without work. A couple in our church read this passage in Acts 4:34–35 during their personal study:

> There was not a needy person among them, for as many as were owners of lands or houses sold them and brought the proceeds of what was sold and laid it at the apostles' feet, and it was distributed to each as any had need.

After reading this verse, they sold some stock they owned and anonymously gave the money to the leadership of our church. That money went on to pay mortgages and grocery bills and electricity for many of the families in our church who were suffering.

Something was sinking in and tangling its way into our hearts and minds and affections. What we once did in order to "matter" or to "be seen" we forgot all about. We matter and are seen because of love. Because there is an object to our actions, we move and love and restore not to matter but because we have been moved, loved, and restored.

Radical acts were not the goal; we were truly moved by a person, in love with him,

> Radical acts were not the goal; we were truly moved by a person, in love with him, with Christ. And out of that love came a willingness to trust and hand over our lives.

with Christ. And out of that love came a willingness to trust and hand over our lives. Out of that, Jesus, because he is merciful, led us to the unique places where we would each give our lives away.

Hundreds of children were sponsored, friends relocated to

impoverished neighborhoods to spread the gospel, friends adopted and fostered, others downsized their homes to give, people reconciled with family members, others forgave and pursued unity in our church, people let go of this life and longed to give themselves away in forgiveness and mercy because of Jesus, because of his forgiveness and mercy.

## led

In Acts 1, Christ had returned to God and promised to give the Holy Spirit. He said essentially, "Don't go anywhere. Don't do anything until he comes."

So they waited, knowing better than to try to change the world in their own little human strength. And then he came; he blew in and everything woke up. Everyone knew what to do and how to do it, where before they were fickle, confused, halfhearted followers.

This was the key to sustained power and impact in average men with mundane lives. Eternity was changed by a few disciples? The entire church age started by fishermen? God was in them—the Holy Spirit. He's given to every person at the moment they put their faith in Christ, but rarely accessed. The Spirit helps us, affirms we are God's, teaches us, even prays for us, leads us in what to do, and equips us with what we need to do it. Here are some examples:

And the Spirit told me to go with them. (Acts 11:12)

And the Spirit said to Philip, "Go over and join this chariot." (Acts 8:29)

"The Helper, the Holy Spirit, whom the Father will send in my name, he will teach you all things and bring to your remembrance all that I said to you." (John 14:26)

"For the Holy Spirit will teach you in that very hour what you ought to say." (Luke 12:12)

This defies our pragmatism. It makes me uncomfortable. I grew up in a conservative Bible church. *Holy Spirit* seemed to mean something out of control and lacking truth. The Holy Spirit *is* truth—how can we miss him throughout the pages of truth, the Bible? Until we believe in the reality of a spiritual war where spiritual beings exist and a spiritual plan is being accomplished, we won't need an invisible Spirit's help. This is ridiculous . . . unless it is all real.

> Until we believe in the reality of a spiritual war where spiritual beings exist and a spiritual plan is being accomplished, we won't need an invisible Spirit's help.

I had made following Christ all about a bunch of rules and principles. But the relationship I'd heard about all that time growing up, this was it. God in me. Leaning into him for self-control when my nine-year-old talks back, for guidance on where to use God's gifts in me, for words when I am fleshing out this book he led me to write, and for patience as the consequences of obeying flooded our lives.

Without the Spirit of God to lead our *anythings*, we will only be do-gooders with our own agendas. And they will fizzle. It will be a phase, some dramatic spiritual experiment we look back on fondly, wishing it had been real life. But sometimes the real thing takes time. We prayed *anything*, but it was over the course of months and years that our *anythings* have been revealed. I imagine this will continue for the rest of our lives; if we remain willing, more *anythings* are in store.

The Spirit now is in us, those bound to Christ, and we wait on him to act. We wait on him to tell us what's next. This is not easy, but it is pretty simple.

## calling home

As I rushed to one of my favorite shops before I left for a meeting in Nashville, I peeked in the window to see if Brooke was working. Brooke was in our small group at church, and she and her husband, Mark, hadn't been married long. While Mark finished grad school, she was managing a darling clothing store in Austin.

I surprised her with a hug as she was closing the register. Her eyes filled up with tears when I asked her how she was. She pulled me over to a corner to tell me about her recent trip home to see her mom. Her mom was diagnosed with multiple sclerosis a few years ago. It was progressing quickly. Her mom never seemed needy or complained, but Brooke saw that her mom needed help; she needed Brooke. As Brooke drove through her hometown, running errands for her mom, she felt the Spirit tugging. Brooke and Mark had been praying *anything*, too, dreaming and willing to give their lives however God called.

> God's priorities are beautiful, and they trickle down into invisible spaces . . . into neighborhoods and families and friends and strangers.

With tears she told me, "Jennie I think my calling is to go home. I wanted it to be orphans or Africa. But God is telling us to go home."

God's priorities are beautiful, and they trickle down into invisible spaces . . . into neighborhoods and families and friends and strangers. He will call us to pour our lives into the cracks around us, and sometimes into cracks far from our doorsteps. But wherever he calls us, we pour, not wishing for a larger crack or a more noticeable one, or even the one we were expecting.

We are watching so many people around us go from consumers to full-on missionaries without changing professions or addresses. For some, their callings were to change those things. But for others it was to notice the need right in front of them.

## dreaming and doing

Oswald Chambers beautifully describes the unique call we each experience:

> The call of God is not a reflection of my nature; my personal desires and temperament are of no consideration. As long as I dwell on my own qualities and traits and think about what I am suited for, I will never hear the call of God. *But when God brings me into the right relationship with Himself,* I will be in the same condition Isaiah was. Isaiah was so attuned to God, because of the great crisis he had just endured, that the call of God penetrated his soul.
>
> The majority of us cannot hear anything but ourselves. And we cannot hear anything God says. *But to be brought to the place where we can hear the call of God is to be profoundly changed.*[10]

In other words, truly knowing our beautiful and terrifying God will make us willing to do *anything.*

Chambers goes on to say,

> Service is the overflow which pours from a life filled with love and devotion. . . . Service is what I bring to the relationship and is the reflection of my identification with the nature of God. Service becomes a natural part of my life. *God brings me into the proper relationship with Himself so that I can understand His call, and then I serve Him on my own out of a motivation of absolute love.* Service to God is the deliberate love-gift of a nature that has heard the call of God. Service is an expression of my nature, and God's call is an expression of His nature. Therefore, when I receive His nature and hear His call,

His divine voice resounds throughout His nature and mine and the two become one in service. The Son of God reveals Himself in me, and out of devotion to Him service becomes my everyday way of life.[11]

Service, or living your *anything*, is simply an expression of what is true about my God: he is trustworthy. I adore my God, and so he has me . . . all of me. I don't choose my own path anymore. It is set for me, laid before the foundations of time. God prepared in advance the good works I would do (Eph. 2:10). That is the beautiful call on my life, on our lives.

Our friends weren't just recklessly saying yes to God's Spirit. They were also being set free from sin they had struggled with for years. As God got bigger, their thousand problems were shrinking. God was setting everyone free. Our affections, our goals, our futures had shifted. We were on a mission. Life was getting really fun because we were running with friends toward heaven.

# PART 3

# living anything

# Jesus' anything

One of the most powerful and intimate views into our Savior's soul can be found in a prayer. It's a prayer that allows us to access the beautiful conversation between Jesus and his father the night before he was to be killed. As we look into the chambers of Christ's soul right before he faced death, we see what most matters to him. It's an example of what he lived for and what we are to live for.

With very different words, Jesus prayed *anything*. He prayed it for himself over and over again in his life, but here he prays it for us during the most crucial event in all of history.

This is what he said to his father on the night before he gave everything for us. Listen to his heart as you read some of his words from that night.

Father, the hour has come; glorify your Son that the Son may glorify you. . . .

I glorified you on earth, having accomplished the work that you gave me to do. . . .

I am glorified in them [those you have given me]. . . .

These things I speak in the world, that they may have my joy fulfilled in themselves.

They are not of the world, just as I am not of the world.

I do not ask that you take them out of the world, but that you keep them from the evil one. . . .

As you sent me into the world, so I have sent them into the world. . . .

Father, I desire that they also, whom you have given me, may be with me where I am, to see my glory that you have given me. (John 17:1, 4, 10, 13–15, 18, 24)

:: 14

# seeing God

## our purpose here

Last week I told Caroline, my almost-six-year-old, to tell me what she wanted for her birthday. I expected her to rattle off a couple items. Instead she disappeared into her room and emerged five minutes later with a detailed list of ten things, compiled with the strategic help of her big brother, who writes faster than she does.

### caroline's birthday list

· An iPod [she did not get an iPod]
· The wooden snake that moves [no idea what this is]
· A real purse
· A wallet
· Leapster games

anything

- A stuffed animal
- A camera—a real one
- Dance Revolution video game [pretty certain this was my older son's addition]
- Sunglasses
- A dog [she did not get a dog]

It was all there just under the surface, a buzzing list of accumulated wishes, things she was pining for, just waiting for me to ask. We sprung for about half this list—the realistic, cheaper half. But impressively, the girl knew exactly what she wanted, with a little help from her brother.

What do I want most?

For me there are so many things. I want a few silly shallow things: I need my car washed right now, and I would love a new iPhone (since mine was recently dropped in the bath) and a night out with my husband or a night to catch up on *30 Rock*. I want deeper things such as close friendships, to be someone my kids would want to be like, and for my words to make a difference. But what do I want most? What's the deepest desire of my soul? I cannot name it, but I am certain it centers entirely around me, a selfish desire to be important or appreciated. Something like that.

What does God want most?

I've always known the answer, though I've never known what the answer meant. I certainly never knew what the answer meant for my life.

God is most after his glory.

*Glory*: it is a vague and mysterious word. John Piper defines God's glory as "the holiness of God put on display."[1] It's who God truly is, being made known so you can see and taste and feel him, and in turn fall flat on your face.

Glory is the evidence of God . . . like his breath on me that night he met me on the bathroom floor. I saw his glory through Katie's blog, and after seeing it, everything about me wanted to change. I wanted to align myself with a God who tasted and felt like that. When I saw God . . . his glory . . . I wanted nothing else. Why did Katie's blog cause God to rush into a soul huddled in Austin, Texas? How did the glory of God fall off a computer screen and into me?

Glory is the evidence of God . . . like his breath on me that night he met me on the bathroom floor.

"Father, the hour has come; glorify your Son that the Son may glorify you . . . I glorified you on earth, having accomplished the work that you gave me to do. . . . I am glorified in them" (John 17:1, 4, 10).

When Jesus went to pray, when he went to meet and plead with his father before facing death, one word fell off his lips over and over again. He prayed for God's *glory*. He longed for it. He said he had spent his life on earth building and displaying it. Nothing mattered more to Jesus before he died than God showing himself through him and through us.

Even as I write these words today, I wonder if I honestly care. I can barely obey God without thinking, *What will it cost me?* I don't want to think that way. Left to myself, I am just that selfish. I want things. I want comfort and fun. I don't want to suffer. I want things to feel in control. Today I don't want to be typing and studying about God's glory—I'd rather be at Target or on Facebook.

Today, like many other days, I have forgotten. I have forgotten my glimpses of God, the moments when I actually taste and see him for a smidge of who he is, and the moments I would do anything. I forget what it feels like to glimpse him as he streams in through a Scripture that

> What if we wanted what God wanted most? What if we wanted, like Jesus, God's glory above every other thing?

surely was written for me. Or as he blows in when I drive with my window down, singing my guts out worshipping, or over yogurt with my nine-year-old as she discovers what it means to embrace the freedom of forgiveness. I have forgotten his glory.

I forget. I forget he is real and that nothing else matters . . . until I see his glory again, marks of him. Then I remember and wake up.

What if we wanted what God wanted most? What if we wanted, like Jesus, God's glory above every other thing?

What if the true motive of my life and my heart were to make God known for a few years on this earth?

## Jesus prays for us

Not only did Jesus pray for himself but he prayed for his disciples and for us.

He said, "They are not of the world, just as I am not of the world . . . As you sent me into the world, so I have sent them into the world" (John 17:16, 18).

The night Jesus prayed this prayer there was no oxygen left in the Upper Room. His death had just been set in motion, he had just told his men he was leaving them, and he had just explained to them that the world would hate them just as the world hated him. Then he prayed this prayer: "Father, glorify yourself through me. Glorify yourself through them" (John 17, paraphrased).

Everyone sitting with him that night felt the weight of a call so large, so costly, so significant: the call to show the glory of God to the earth. A few men meant to display God. Eventually, most of those men were killed for this call.

Jesus went on to pray, "I do not ask for these only, but also for those who will believe in me through their word" (John 17:20). He also said, "I am no longer in the world, but they are in the world" (John 17:11).

Friends, we're up. Those men are gone. Now we show God. But we would rather be at Target or on Facebook.

## simple, not easy

Jessie was one of those girls who you meet and you know she would be a great friend. She is disarming and real and easy. I love spending time with her. She and some of her friends were new to following Christ. They had been burned with legalism and had avoided the church most of their lives. But a lot of them hoped for a God, and through the pursuit of some Christian coworkers, Jessie and her friends found themselves in our living room, learning more about Jesus. They sat discovering a God that seemed bigger than they'd thought. They sat with hungry eyes, asking questions like, "So the Bible is not in chronological order?" "Who is the Holy Spirit?" "Where did God come from?" They were trying to unpack a new God. And they could not write down the answers fast enough.

They were starving for more and more understanding of him, this God who blew their previous categories, for whom they could stop trying to measure up. He was beautiful to them.

On this night, Jessie asked if she could stay late. I knew she was wrestling. You could see it in her eyes. She sat down with Zac and me in our living room and went on to tell us that her boyfriend had asked her to move in with him. She had said yes. They were eventually going to get married when they could afford it. Her parents even thought it was a good idea to try out life together before committing. And so did she—until she met God. Now she wasn't sure.

Zac and I listened and marveled as this new believer was discovering that her God lived inside of her, undid her, led her, and moved her.

I hadn't addressed sex or marriage much yet. This was God moving her. And she had to decide.

Was she all in? Was God worth it?

If she was all in, telling her boyfriend was going to be the hardest thing she'd ever had to do.

She left that night with a plan to not only tell him that she wasn't going to live with him but also that she wanted to stop having sex until they were married. We never told her what to do. We sat in awe of this movement of the Spirit of God in her, calling her to her own costly *anything*.

We prayed for her, and she left our house that night so heavy and so afraid. She was about to risk all she had on a God who had not even occurred to her a few months prior, departing from a world full of conventional wisdom and practical choices.

Jesus says, "They are not of the world, just as I am not of the world" (John 17:16). But I wake up in this world every morning, and my feet land in pretty much the same place on my carpet. Located close to the carpet where my feet land are a lot of dirty dishes, two cars that need gas, a lawn that needs to be mowed, a stack of bills, and a bunch of kids who need to eat. See, we wake up every day to a world that needs us. All people everywhere are waking up and setting their feet on the earth, with their own sets of responsibilities that are likely defined by whether their feet land on tile or wood or carpet or dirt.

But we all wake up and put our feet down every day, and we move through our time here according to the rules, expectations, demands, and hopes of our given space in this world. The given place in which I grew up issued a script that spelled out a life lived near family, in a safe neighborhood where you had a fence and cute curtains, and where life wasn't too hard, especially if you loved Jesus.

But Jesus prayed this for me, and the same for all of us who would come to know him:

*You are not of this world, Jennie. You don't belong here. You are going to put your feet down every morning in this world, but you don't belong to it. You don't adhere to its rules and expectations. You don't even hope for the same things. Because you know me and you are mine, your home, your hope is with me forever. Your expectations are that your short life here is spent on my mission even if it is costly. Because you know it is short.*

I keep forgetting that life is temporary—so temporary. I place my hope in this life and I build for it and live for it. I came across this tweet from Tyler Merrick, creator of Project 7 Coffee, a company whose profits are given to the least of these all over the world. He wrote, "If life is temporary, why create the safest one possible that gets you through it with the least amount of scars?"[2]

> If we believe this life is temporary, that belief alone changes how we live it.

If we believe this life is temporary, that belief alone changes how we live it.

The morning after Jessie nervously left our living room to tell her boyfriend she wouldn't live with him, I got an incredibly long text. I assumed their relationship wouldn't make it through this. I just thought her boyfriend, Matt, would never understand. Part of me thought God's timing seemed poor. I hated that God might cost her so much so early. To quote my daughter Kate, they were just getting to know each other, Jessie and God. And yet he was asking her to potentially walk away from the most important person to her.

We don't follow God just because he is God, just because he is boss. We follow God because he builds beautiful stories, even if they are not easy. Jessie's text read:

anything

Last night I was so nervous, but I told Matt everything we talked about, everything I was feeling about God. Matt listened and then he told me that God had been moving in him too. He was also convicted and wanted to please God with our relationship but he had been scared to tell me.

Together they began growing and pursuing purity. In the months that followed, I would see them sitting in church together, so peaceful and so happy. God was real, and in living for him, they were finding a story that was not easy—but it was beautiful. If Jessie had not risked and obeyed her new invisible God, they would have missed so much.

> Christ never intended those who walked with him to feel comfortable and safe. This was meant to be a risk-it-all pursuit.

If we pray anything, we will all, like Christ, be called to give up this life and things we love. We will be called to risk for his glory. Christ never intended those who walked with him to feel comfortable and safe. This was meant to be a risk-it-all pursuit. The glory of God will be made great on this earth, but what a privilege to be part of his plan to restore it.

How did God's glory fall off a computer screen and into me? Because a young girl writing a blog in Africa was living the story God wrote for her. She had surrendered and obeyed, and in turn I glimpsed the glory of God.

# blast off

## overcoming doubts

Everything was moving faster, as if we had been slowly cranking to the top of our roller coaster, grappling with our fear and unknowns, and now we were about to free fall.

In July, the night before my thirty-second birthday, God woke me up in the middle of the night. While God had been clear in calling me to use my gifts, I very much assumed that was in the context of our church and community. So I had been writing and teaching a Bible study called *Stuck*. It was a study born out of my own struggles and the freedom I was finding as God was prying my fingers off of my life. *Stuck* was helping us all process how Jesus intersects with all the invisible things we struggle with, like discontentment and anger and fear.

However, as I was teaching on fear, I was living it right in front of them, doing my best to get over my own fear of being so exposed while teaching and writing. There was no denying that God was using this. People were growing and giving their lives away and finding freedom. Women were questioning their nominal faith, and others were accepting Christ for the first time. It was beautiful. This was not just producing more knowledge; God was using it to produce obedience. We were all changing.

But the night before my birthday, God woke me up. I thought I was stepping out and doing what he wanted, so I wasn't brainstorming further. I was already more exposed than I was comfortable with. But God had more, and that night he gave me my next assignment.

> I was already more exposed than I was comfortable with. But God had more, and that night he gave me my next assignment.

He gave me a vision that our generation would start giving him away rather than just learning about him. He wanted me to call and then equip women who already know and love God to gather friends, coworkers, neighbors, and others into conversations—experiences centered on God. God was calling all of us who were spoiled with so much truth to live that truth and to give it away to those who may not have ever attended church or a more traditional Bible study.

In Luke 14 Jesus tells a story that captivates me. This story is the call of our God, his heart for the lost and the suffering.

A man once gave a great banquet and invited many. And at the time for the banquet he sent his servant to say to those who had been invited, "Come, for everything is now ready." But they all alike began to make excuses. So the servant came and reported these things to his master. Then the master of the house became angry and said to his servant, "Go out quickly to the streets and lanes of the city, and bring in the poor and crippled and blind and lame."

And the servant said, "Sir, what you commanded has been done, and still there is room." (vv. 16–22)

And here is where I get teary . . .

And the master said to the servant, "Go out to the highways and hedges and *compel people to come in, that my house may be filled.*" (v. 23, emphasis added)

Our God is compelling. He is asking us to go compel people to him. To *compel* means to have a powerful or irresistible influence in the lives of others.

Many of us don't do this much. We avoid compelling anyone to God because it may feel cheesy or annoying. Well then, we have to find ways to compel that aren't cheesy or annoying. The problem with this new generation and their endearing disgust for "faking it" is that they run from church and organized religion. So, we'll have to take God to them.

> We avoid compelling anyone to God because it may feel cheesy or annoying. Well then, we have to find ways to compel that aren't cheesy or annoying.

I was already teaching the *Stuck* study, and something about it felt different—something that God was calling me to expand. He was using *Stuck* to cross over and bring people together of all ages and struggles, and I knew my assignment would start there. Maybe these experiences could bridge the gap between deep believers and those just considering God.

I woke up the morning of my birthday and I did not respond like Mary rejoicing . . . I just felt ill. I knew it had been from God. I knew I had already agreed to do it months earlier when Zac and I prayed *anything* and God had hinted that he was taking me this way. And now the weight and enormity of this was getting clearer. I am not one of those girls who wants to be famous. I hate the attention even from being the pastor's wife in our community. And I knew, for this vision, I would have to put myself out there on a larger scale. It made me laugh and then it made me sick. I had three kids and another about to come and fill our extra bed. How was I supposed to catch the attention of a publisher, much less a generation?

My closest friends took me away for the night to celebrate my birthday. Bekah, my dear friend who found her Africa at home by sharing Christ with her neighbors, made my favorite dessert. We were sitting around the pool above the skyline of Austin and eating trifle. Knowing me as well as they do, my friends know that the best gift for me is to go deep fast. Food combined with rich conversation is some measure of heaven to me. So, they started peppering me with probing questions.

> God knew I could never do this alone. He always gives us what we need to accomplish his purposes.

Unable to hold in how heavy I felt, I cried to them about waking up with this vision, the fear, the unknowns, and the call. Seeing my reluctance, they wisely just listened, encouraging me, "Jennie, you have to do it" and "God will do this. Don't worry. Just wait." They affirmed my gifts and this call but helped me wait patiently for God to move.

That group of friends has gone on to hold me up as this call has fleshed itself out. They gather to pray for me regularly, they text me Scripture when I feel inadequate, they celebrate with me, and, when I have many times wanted to say no and stop the chaos, they have pushed me further into obedience. God knew I could never do this alone. He always gives us what we need to accomplish his purposes.

In the days and months that followed, I didn't go out and miraculously get picked up by the perfect publisher. I just sat. Honestly, I wanted to let my *anything* play out in caring for my kids and loving the people close to me as best I could. Maybe I could answer this calling later, at fifty . . .

I knew that if God wanted me to do something more, I would need to wait on him to pull it off. I did not want to create something and then wonder if it had been me or God. I would obey as he revealed the next step, and, in the meantime, live as faithfully as I could through the typical stuff.

So, in the fall, I went on teaching a new study on the life of David and what it looked like to completely abandon your life to God and chase after him. I think the women in that study felt as though they were watching their teacher struggle trying to figure out God, just as David had. I was a wreck and passionate and teary and sold out. I just got up there in front of them and bled and cried. But nothing new came in that time . . .

During that study, I saw some things in David I hadn't seen before. I saw his eyes—they were laser focused on God. He had a disaster of a life, but every time his eyes veered, he quickly and instinctively refocused them on his God. This pleased God so much that he would run his future kingdom through David, calling him a man after his own heart. This screwed up, laser-focused guy pleased God.

I let God's writing assignment simmer in the background for the time being, and I felt my heart chasing after one of the other *anythings* he had prepared for our family. After reading Katie's blog and getting the "empty bed" hint from God after Zac and I prayed, I wanted to get to Africa and get the ball rolling. I wanted to see for myself, thinking that God might make the next step clearer if we could meet these kids face-to-face. We knew we were supposed to fill that bed, but we were just still so afraid. I wrote this at the time:

*Curtains and Cute Lives*
August 6, 2009

If you have followed my blog in the last few months, you know that we have been wrestling about the plans God has for us for our short time here. We have been willing to do anything, terribly aware that we will only be here for a little while and wanting God to use us in that time.

But when I started this blog I was not even to that place fully. I believed I would use this space to share what I was learning in a transparent way. I had no idea that God was about to stir things in my heart that were slightly beyond my realms of "normal."

> My life is not my own, and I write to give away what I have been given.

Yet here I am blogging, and here we are dreaming. And I am torn. I began this blog with the conviction that every entry would be a glimpse into my heart and current struggles, no matter how rough. And yet sharing honestly about my struggles with these dreams seems potentially inappropriate—like I am lifting the curtain to our most private things, possibly opening my inner life up to dozens of opinions.

But maybe the timing of this blog and our wrestlings is no accident. Maybe this is what God wants to use. My life is not my own, and I write to give away what I have been given. I write with no shame, fully disclosing my inadequate humanity and God's upheaval of my wreck of a heart and head, knowing full well it is the plight of every believer. God would be about undoing us on every issue of the heart. So, if I make mine public, I sincerely need your grace.

Writer and theologian Henri Nouwen said it this way: "It is my growing conviction that my life belongs to others just as much as it belongs to myself and that what is experienced as most unique often proves to be most solidly embedded in the common condition of being human."[3]

I am counting on only fellow humans reading this, and we will see if my muddled process with the God of the universe is actually quite common.

If I could save a life, at no risk to my own, would I not do it? This is the position we find ourselves in. We are rich (in light of most of the world) and situated and comfortable with a bed to spare and a usually full pantry, and yet I feel scared. I am brought to tears at the sight of almost any picture from Africa. I think of a child over there who could be ours, already born and not yet claimed, and what am I waiting for? I don't know—but I am scared for how our lives will change with the many unknowns. I worry about the white world we would be bringing a child into. I wonder about having four kids. (Unlike my sisters, I never wanted more than three kids.) Our lives seem so full—usually overflowing.

We have not begun the paperwork yet, but some days we feel close. Of course, some people think we are foolish for pursuing this. But I am realizing that goes with almost any act of recklessness, even reckless love. When Zac and I left the movie theater after *The Proposal* (of all movies) he said, "That made me want to adopt . . . it was about a woman who was unloved and so she didn't know how to love . . . and we have enough love in our home for this." He always says, "Why would we not?" On most days I agree.

I can't forget about these kids who have no one and nothing in the world—and I have everything, including the capacity to help at least one of them. Why would I not save a life at no risk to my own? Or is this a risk to my life . . . my familiar, safe life? It could only be a risk to our comfort . . . not my life. Some think we need to be 100 percent sure before we do this . . . saying, "Is God really calling you?" But I think God does not have to over-clarify for us to obey. God has said his piece . . . Does he will for me to take my ridiculous abundance and bless others in need? Does he want me to care for the poor? Does he want me to lay down my life? Did he command me to care for orphans? God's clarity is not my issue.

One thing big—God must replace the chaos of me. I'm over my cute, comfortable, easy life. I don't want to make decisions based on my adequacy and capacity. I don't want to miss what God has for us because I am afraid.[4]

Just because we were willing didn't mean it was easy. I still wanted God to be more clear, so we could be more sure. I asked a friend who had adopted if they were 100 percent sure when they adopted their two kids from Rwanda. I expected her to say yes; instead she laughed out loud, hard. She said, "Of course we weren't sure. At some point you just jump, doubting, all the way down."

## blind okays

So I made my plans to go on a vision trip to Rwanda. Our church was about to get involved in ministry over there, and they needed a scouting team. Of course I jumped. But right before it was time to go, my husband came home and said, "Hey—I am going to take your place on that trip. I need to go."

Crushed but trusting, I handed my dream over to Zac.

In January 2010, the week of the horrifying earthquake in Haiti, Zac went to what I had come to think of as my Africa. But God let the world see the orphans' faces that week in a way that defies words. Every night my husband was gone, I fell asleep watching the dark little faces on TV of children in Haiti with no one. I think the whole world wanted to adopt after that week. I, too, was ready.

After one visit to the Rwandan orphanage, Zac called it. On a poor connection over Skype he told me, "Jennie, we are adopting."

And this time I was the one to say, "Okay."

# out of control

## God in the chaos

A year and a half had passed since I said "okay" over a static-filled connection to Zac in Africa. The paperwork had long since been completed. Somewhere in that time, my husband sent me to a writer's conference where I met an agent who wanted to represent me, and somehow, months later I had a publisher with a contract to write several studies in line with the vision God had given me years earlier. They also wanted me to write books. I knew what my first book would be. I was living it.

God was writing a story for my life I never would have written.

Things like this don't just happen. God was writing a story for my life I never would have written. Even as I type this, I don't know how he did it or why I have a privilege of writing about my God, but I am so glad he trumped me, even though all of this—even typing these words—is the scariest thing to me.

⠿ ⠿
⠿ ⠿

My friend Laura was settled now completely into her faith and the tables had turned. She was now the one counseling me and encouraging me in my own crisis. I ordered lunch; Laura kept looking down at her tiny baby bundle. She slept perfectly; her dark skin glowed, tucked in to a little carrier with her black curls falling around her little frilly ribbon. Laura glowed too. As I thanked God for the food, I flashed back to conversations we had shared years ago when Laura was lost and confused, dangling over the edge of her skyscraper, jaded by some other god that was not real, a god that had bound her with rules and fears and insecurity.

Laura now sat in front of me full of life and purpose and a real God. Her little African angel was physically transforming before our eyes. Good food and too much love were beginning to bring life to her little body, even her soul . . . you could see that when she opened her poppy little brown eyes. The baby was full and content. Everything had changed. Everything had changed for both of them. Their lives were screaming of a God too good to ever leave.

Both Laura and the baby had crossed over in some way. Both were crossing from death to life. Both had found a home. I finished thanking God for great food, a great friend, and for the way he creatively and intentionally redeems us. As I said amen, I felt the weight in my chest growing. It had been there for months. We were supposed to have our child by now. We had thought we would get our son in Rwanda with Laura, but we had not heard a word from the Rwandan government. As happy as I was to see Laura and her gorgeous daughter, my own stomach was in knots. After a year and a half of waiting, there were signs that the little boy we were getting was not well. His legs were braced for reasons we did not know . . . could it be degenerative? But we could not get to him yet. We were helpless.

Every time I thought about him there, in the orphanage with no one to tuck him in or wrap him up in a warm towel after baths or make sure that he was going to bed fed, I would start to spin out. My mind trusted God, but my heart frantically grasped for a solution that did not exist. The government would tell us when we could go, and they seemed in no hurry.

> My mind trusted God, but my heart frantically grasped for a solution that did not exist.

Numbness had become my default, my mode of coping with all that was unfolding and the reality of my deteriorating child. Would he be able to walk? So many other things were pressing in with new uncertainties. Zac and the elders had been wrestling with the future of the church, which meant the future of our home. My writing and ministry were taking on a life of their own. God had been clear about his will for our lives, but they still felt completely out of control.

## push back

In parenting, at some point you give in to the lack of control. Most of us fight this in the beginning, scheduling feedings and outings and packing the perfect diaper bag, but then you have two or maybe three babies who turn into toddlers. At some point you either live perpetually anxious or give in and embrace the fact that your life is now completely out of your control.

Once you embrace that, parenting shifts from an agenda to an experience. You start relishing dirty floors and tantrums and potty training, even though it is hard and taxing and impossible to contain. You still train your kids, but somehow you learn to let it all play out rather than trying so hard to smash it and them into perfect compliance. You realize that the phrase *well-behaved toddler* is an oxymoron. When strangers look disapprovingly at your kid's behavior in public, you learn to say things like, "We are in process," rather than secretly pinching your kid under the table.

I think that is a good analogy for what happened when Zac and I prayed *anything*. I was anxious and trying to control this life, and so concerned with outcomes that weren't ever in my control to begin with. I was so concerned with how it was all appearing.

And then we let go. We shifted. We gave in.

And while it was hard . . . it was simple. God was in control. He was real. He saw us. And we were going to eventually or quickly get to heaven with him. See, we weren't going to be here very long. And everything we did between now and when we met him was up to him.

## baby anythings

Laura's new baby was still asleep, so she began pressing in with deep questions over lunch, as annoyingly good friends always do. I felt the lump growing in my throat and pushed away the feelings I had been pushing away every day for months. If I went there, if I let it all in, I was sure our lunch would be over. So I redirected the subject in an effort to redirect the force of emotion about to undo me.

Then the phone rang. It was Zac. I let it go to voicemail thinking I would call him when we were finished. One minute later he called again. Laura paused.

I answered, "Hey. What's up?"

"Rwanda called. He is ours. Let's go to Africa."

Laura and I both blinked back tears. I couldn't wrap my brain around it. After a year and a half, was it really our turn? If it was, I had a lot to do. The past few months had been full of work and writing and filming for the *Stuck* study, and we'd been preparing a room and a family for what was ahead.

Right after lunch I got on the phone with my editor, and we tore through the rest of our to-do list. There was still so much left to do. I was coming off on the phone as unemotional, even calloused. She stopped me and said, "Jennie, are you okay?" I didn't know. I was spinning.

Our faith, the fact that we had stepped out and trusted an invisible God, was about to be tested. Within a few months our lives would not resemble the lives we had before we prayed. It wasn't just our new son; every category of our lives was undone and released. Every thought was laid on top of the pressing reality of a pending eternity with our God. We weren't the same.

By moving forward into a call to a more public ministry, I was not going to get to hide and enjoy everyone's approval. Plus, we were choosing to adopt a four-year-old toddler who had been raised thus far in an orphanage in Africa . . . not exactly the safest, most predictable route to building the perfect family.

> Once God was free in our lives, he was loud and clear, and following him was not that complicated. Especially because he kept showing up.

So this wasn't the easy road, but it felt really simple. Once God was free in our lives, he was loud and clear, and following him was not that complicated. Especially because he kept showing up.

But a collision was coming. God was calling me to a seemingly demanding ministry at the same time that we would be getting our toddler son from Rwanda—and of course maintaining our already chaotic life. God was beginning to stir up other things, too, with Zac's job, the church, and our future. I kept waiting for something to fall through. Was there about to be a major train wreck? Or were all these God callings going to merge and beautifully work together?

We had long since gotten over building a comfy, easy life and were completely surrendered to God, but not everyone looking in understood. And like us, they could see the collision coming.

Kim had asked if we could meet. As we sat sipping coffee, I sensed she had something pressing to say. And she did. She loved us—and she was also a fairly sane and practical person.

"Jennie, I am worried about you. Is all this wise? Aren't you asking for trouble? I just don't think you can handle all this. I think you and Zac really need to consider how much adoption and your new ministry may change your lives."

I listened and nodded. Everything in me was receiving what she was saying. I was scared too. And my doubts and reluctance were always with me. I wanted easy more than they all wanted easy for us, except . . .

Kim wasn't the only person questioning our increasingly reckless life. We were getting these questions a lot. These were people we trust and love, and they love God too. So we had to listen and consider what they were saying. Our families were especially worried, constantly bringing up their concerns and fears. Their opinions mattered deeply to us. We longed for their support.

> God was in all of this . . . all of the chaos he was initiating in beautiful ways.

So we did listen. Over and over again Zac and I would go over their concerns and pray, but there was one thing we could never shake.

God had been markedly clear. Clear like he's never been before to both of us. And most of the people who had seen all of it up close . . . all the little places God had entered and filled and led during these processes . . . they all knew it was supernatural. God was in all of this . . . all of the chaos he was initiating in beautiful ways.

So we would pray and struggle and lay everything, again, back at the feet of God. And he would remind us of all he had already done and the unspeakable peace that we both felt, even with the people close to us doubting, even with the difficulty growing, not shrinking.

I wrote this as we were processing.

April 15th, 2010

We are getting a lot of fair, loving questions right now such as,

"How are you going to do all of this? Adopt, be a pastor's wife, write and speak, manage your kids' lives, be a good friend, and on and on?"

I don't know. I tear up as I write this because God knows I have told him, "Do your will. I don't care about any of it, unless you want us to do it." And he has overwhelmingly affirmed us both to move forward in adoption and writing and teaching, and he seems to want us to keep our other three kids too.

But I am just me.

I am not fancy and able. At the end of the day I am just me. And I worry, just as everyone close to me right now does, about my family and all of this he is calling me to do.

But this is my hope.

"Now may the God of peace who brought again from the dead our Lord Jesus, the great shepherd of the sheep, by the blood of the eternal covenant, *equip you with everything good that you may do his will, working in us that which is pleasing in his sight, through Jesus Christ, to whom be glory forever and ever.* Amen." (Hebrews 13:20–21, emphasis added)[5]

We knew.

We knew God was calling us not only to obey him but to trust him with whatever the consequences of our obedience would be.

Our coffee had grown lukewarm. Kim sat waiting to hear my response to her concerns. I whispered the only thing I could:

> We have become such a pragmatic society with our pros and cons and schedules that when we get to matters of radical obedience, it's easy for us to talk ourselves out of it.

"But how do we disobey God? We have to obey because *he is God*. He gets to say what we do now. He will take care of us. He'll take care of our kids and us. We know this is going to be hard. But we are trusting that he's going to help us navigate whatever is ahead."

We have become such a pragmatic society with our pros and cons and schedules that when we get to matters of radical obedience, it's easy for us to talk ourselves out of it. We rationalize that if the cost outweighs the benefit, then we shouldn't do it.

God's Word in 1 Corinthians 1 says:

"For the word of the cross is folly to those who are perishing, but to us who are being saved it is the power of God. . . . Has not God made foolish the wisdom of the world?" (1:18, 20)

Those of us who know Christ, we live for a different reality. We live for things we can't see and make decisions based on that different reality. Our reality is a cross, a heaven, and a God who sees us and gives us his Spirit so we can do something while we are here. And that's not building a cute, easy life for ourselves where the pros outweigh the cons.

We build for him.

"As you sent me into the world, so I have sent them into the world" (John 17:18). We get after it; we obey because we are his representatives here. We are God's hands here. That means something. That does things to you.

It makes you live for things you can't see yet.

I sat on the concrete steps overlooking a patch of grass where my kids were playing soccer. Behind them was the landscape of a place that had claimed my heart before I ever laid eyes on it. A place that had weathered the deadliest genocide only a few years prior. And yet it was a place that perhaps was full of more joy and beauty than I had ever seen. Its very landscape declared there is a God who redeems.

I sat watching as my oldest son kicked a Rwandan soccer ball to his new little brother. Cooper's dark skin only highlighted his brilliant, imperfect smile. They had a few common languages going between them: sports and laughter and outdoors and brotherhood. It had only been twenty-four hours since he had become ours, and yet I knew that no matter what challenges lay ahead, this could be the most beautiful story of my life.

Tears came as I felt God whispering, *Jennie, what if you had been too afraid to obey me?*

*Look at what you would have missed.*

# war on

## fighting brave

There are always doubts. We doubt because God, while he gets louder, is still invisible, because of the people questioning your sanity and the difficulty of just following a wild invisible God into uncomfortable spaces. We doubt because of the risk, the cost, the abandonment of rights and comforts, the disapproval of people you really love, and then on top of it all, because you have now officially picked a fight with the devil.

Yep. Fun.

The devil is real, and nothing ticks him off more than people waking up from the numb stupor he has crafted to keep us

> The devil is real, and nothing ticks him off more than people waking up from the numb stupor he has crafted to keep us harmless.

harmless. Zac and I were awake and running and single-mindedly chasing God, and that got the devil's attention.

We've served God long enough to experience attack. In fact, we came to expect it in the early years of church planting. Zac and I eventually would stop whatever irrational fight we were having and laugh, blame it on the devil, and call a truce. But we were in new territory. The devil stepped up his game.

In a matter of months, on top of all the new change coming and the weight of it all, we experienced:

- the worst fights of our marriage;
- friends betraying us;
- one of our other kids going through uncommon behavior issues at school;
- out-of-the-blue temptations that had never previously been issues;
- our church going through more conflict than we had ever seen;
- and other things that are not mine to share.

Every day Zac (when we weren't fighting) would look at me and hug me and then he would say, "Are we right with God?" If the answer was yes then he would ask, "Then how do we obey him in this new hard thing?"

And the answer was usually clear. Honestly, I could handle all of the hard stuff until we were at odds with each other. Zac had been my rock in all of this. I leaned on him to support me through the weighty callings on our lives. He and I were unified until this point. Losing that unity made me question everything.

I had just spent the hardest week of my life pouring my guts out on camera for the *Stuck* study. It was one of the scariest and most intense things I'd ever done. One night, it felt as if the attacks had come so hard for so many weeks that I locked myself in my bathroom not to cry . . . but to cuss. I was mad. I punched the air as though the devil was so real I might hit him. And I begged God for reprieve.

"Do you see us? We are getting our butts kicked! Can you get in here, please, and issue some backup? We are dying!"

We were pouring ourselves out and getting attacked from every side. I needed it to let up. I was losing perspective and I needed to breathe. I just had it out.

It should not surprise us if life is hard, especially if we love Jesus. We are at war—not in heaven. And yet it always does surprise us.

## braveheart fantasies

Jesus prayed before he died, asking God to use us here. He sent us on God's mission to redeem and love and pursue and protect and heal. Jesus said that he was going but he was leaving these men, and the ones who would believe in him because of them, to continue his mission . . . but there would be attack. He said, "I do not ask that you take them out of the world, but that you keep them from the evil one" (John 17:15).

When you are truly about the things of God, there is always attack.

So Jesus prayed for us, not that we would be kept from hardship or suffering but that we would be kept from the evil one who desires to take us out.

How many times have I kicked and pouted to God because life was not going how I wanted? How many times have I thought to myself, *That is not fair!*

While I may have read in my Bible that we are in a spiritual war, that truth had not fully adjusted my expectations of this life. To accept that life is supposed to be hard is the beginning of joy.

There is freedom in understanding that heaven is coming and we are not there yet. We're called to live, instead, aware that we are at war with a ruthless enemy who is trying to destroy us if we are living surrendered to Jesus.

It reminds me of *Gone with the Wind*. Scarlett O'Hara is a little diva before the war. Her food is brought in to her extravagant bedroom on silver trays. But when she gets home to Tara after the war, she gets her hoe in the dirt and tries to get corn to grow, telling everyone around her to quit complaining. Because of the war, her reality was different, and therefore she lived differently. She went from pouty and spoiled to an intense work horse.

But honestly, I think most people are craving something bigger than comfort and an easy life. I think, if you are still reading this book, you are someone who feels that. You might watch movies and shows such as *Braveheart* or *Band of Brothers* and you realize there is something deeply moving about war, about fighting for something worthy of death, about living lives that matter for something big. I think we watch those things and long to participate in something bigger than PTA and cheering for the Mavs. I think God wrote that into our souls. We were made for this bigger story . . . we were made to show the glory of God and to fight dark cosmic forces, even if we are at PTA or a Mavs game. I know—it still sounds insane to me too.

We were made for this bigger story . . . we were made to show the glory of God and to fight dark cosmic forces.

We have one foot on the earth and one foot in heaven. We're present here, not taken out of this world but living for another. We're fighting for God's glory and clinging to him for protection and guidance.

Ephesians 6 is clear about this war: "Put on the whole armor of God, that you may be able to stand against the schemes of the devil" (v. 11).

God begins in Ephesians 6 by telling us something like this: *First, remember who you are fighting. You're not fighting flesh and blood, the people hurting you, their sting—you are not fighting them. You are fighting rulers and authorities and cosmic powers over this present darkness. You are fighting the forces of evil in heavenly places.*

Seriously.

I grew up thinking that it was not very Christian to talk about the devil too much. What the heck?! I think it matters. I think when cosmic evil dark forces are fighting you . . . it is good to at least have a heads-up.

It changes the way you live; it changes the way you fight. Maybe it makes you need God. In the bathroom, punching the air, I needed a rescuer. I needed my God.

We are not fighting flesh and blood; we are fighting arrows launched into us by dark forces who want to annihilate us. It helped me be more able to forgive when I realized we never are really fighting people. My friends, my husband, they love God and love me, but the devil knows if I feel alone, unsafe with people in our church, unsafe at home with my husband, I quickly unravel. Again, it's like the war in *Band of Brothers*. They went through hell, but having each other made it bearable. Forgiveness becomes easier when I realize people are not my enemies.

God has bigger purposes in allowing us to suffer, bigger than just winning. He allows us to suffer because we change through suffering.

Something about war makes us better. We live more thankful, less numb. We aren't quite so spoiled. See, God has bigger purposes in allowing us to suffer, bigger than just winning. He allows us to suffer because we change through suffering. We hurt with others better. We become humble. We want him more. "Count it all joy, my brothers, when you meet trials of various kinds, for you know that the testing of your faith produces steadfastness" (James 1:2–3).

Honestly, we grow up through suffering. And most of us need to grow up. I've learned to quit wishing away the hard stuff, because I don't want to miss all the good stuff that goes with it.

Zac and I made up. He is my best friend again, but we continue to walk through attacks. We will all continue to face discouragement, loneliness, criticism, and suffering.

And here is what I hear God speaking to me in it.

*You protect yourself with me.*

*You bind truth to the front of you so when darkness comes you remember me. You remember I am bigger. You remember I win. You remember I am with you today and forever; even if you can't see me, I am there. You put my Word, my truth, in front of you. Protect yourself with me and my righteousness.*

*And then, you run. Let your feet carry you into battle building my name, sharing my love, telling my story, showing my glory. Go. Run. Fight. Do not just sit there feeling sorry for yourself. Run and fight.*

*Let your shield be faith. See, if I am real to you—if you believe you stand behind the God of universes—you won't need to be afraid. You may get tired but you won't forget why this war matters if you don't forget me. You'll fight bravely, like someone who knows she fights for a cause worth dying for. You'll keep fighting if you see me.*

*You have me with you—I am in you.*

*Fight bravely because I am for you and I am with you.*

# backward

## where freedom hides

As we went through the agonizing wait to meet my son Cooper, I read several books about his country, Rwanda. One of the books was titled *We Wish to Inform You That Tomorrow We Will Be Killed with Our Families.*[6] That was the name of the book. I would sit up at night with knots in my stomach as I read about one of the most horrifying events to ever take place.

It tells the story of a man killing his neighbor, with whom he had drinks weeks earlier, and then systematically killing his neighbor's wife and every one of his children. Rwandans burned churches full of women and children who had been trying to hide and then listening to their screams as they burned. There were nearly one million people killed in one hundred days.

I read books; I even watched movies. I needed to—I wanted to be able to pass on Rwandan history and heritage to my future son because that place would always be a part of him. Then, finally, we went.

Before we met Cooper, as we got off the plane in Rwanda, four friends welcomed us—Rwandan men my husband knew: our driver, a counselor who worked with the street kids ministry we supported, our attorney who had helped us with the adoption, and our adoption advocate.

Four strong, handsome, dark men welcomed us into their beautiful and complicated country. As I reached to shake their hands, they hugged me instead and laughed with jolly, warm laughs. I was so struck by these men and their joy and passion that I teared up just at their welcome.

What special men who radiate joy in the midst of marked and suffering lives.

But in this country, these weren't unusual men. Almost every person I met in Rwanda loved well and overflowed with joy. While I was going to college and pledging a sorority, these men and women's loved ones were slaughtering or being slaughtered, and today most of them were still living in poverty—and yet they were flooded with joy and peace and passion.

> We want joy, passion, love, and peace. Every one of us.

Was I really taking my son to a better place?

We all want what those four men have, what that country held. We want joy, passion, love, and peace. Every one of us.

We read books looking for it. We get married hoping for it. We have sex to find it. We climb ladders reaching for it. We have kids in search of it. We look for friends to give it. We spend way too much money at the Apple store trying to buy it. We check e-mails looking for it.

And yet it seems to escape us. Joy, passion, love, and peace. Instead we seem marked by fear, insecurity, apathy, restlessness.

Is it possible we have it all backward?

## lost life

"For whoever would save his life will lose it, but whoever loses his life for my sake will find it" (Matt. 16:25).

"Whoever loves his life loses it, and whoever hates his life in this world will keep it for eternal life" (John 12:25).

Freedom is tucked away, hidden in verses like these. Jesus is whispering, *I am the way. I am truth. I am life* (John 14:6). Freedom and healing hide in the backward way God tells us to find life.

Die to live. Lose to find. Empty yourself to be filled.

I never expected that in one major act of obedience, dying to this life, everything in me would shift. It is not as if I don't feel those things anymore. I am still a mess of a girl . . . ask my husband. But there was a shift.

I remember when it occurred to me how much had changed. It was only the day after the bathroom floor, as if God was eager to point out how much he can change a soul yielded totally to him. I received a very condemning e-mail from someone in our church. It was incredibly hurtful to me. It ordinarily would have sent me crawling to bed in tears. But when I braced for the weight of shame and insecurity that descends on my shoulders when I fail to please people, instead, I felt God's voice leading me, *Apologize and let her go.*

Die to live.
Lose to find.
Empty yourself
to be filled.

For years, I had known what I should do but could not seem to control my heart to do it. I could hear good advice, even godly advice, but I couldn't seem to stop my heart from feeling the out-of-control feelings of fear and insecurity and pride.

How does one control the heart?

Jesus prayed before he died, *You live for this other world, you live my mission, you glorify me here by obeying my voice and my Word, and you fight well, and I am telling you all of this because I want you to have joy.*

"These things I speak in the world, that they may have my joy fulfilled in themselves" (John 17:13).

Joy comes from giving yourself entirely and unreservedly to God.

Like ripping a Band-Aid off, giving in, yielding everything, and dying to this life and all we think we want in it—something about that sets you free.

Everything I was worried about didn't seem so important.

Everything I was afraid of didn't seem that scary.

Everything I wanted before seemed trite.

Everything I doubted about God seemed foolish.

Instead, I felt as though God had placed me in a new reality; a new story that would climax when I met him face-to-face in heaven; a story where he had important things for me if I would listen and obey; a story where he was the main character and I would follow his lead, where I'd never feel more at peace than when playing that role.

If I could remember this today, something could happen. Something so much greater than my feeling important or appreciated, greater than Target and status updates, even greater than healthy kids and a happy life. I could watch God stream through me, pour out of me, move me and move others, and remind us all of something big. Something real. Something we could participate in that actually would last and matter.

Prayers like *anything* place us in the midst of stories. These stories have an author who writes characters, places, and parts. He develops story lines that are actually quite epic, even if they feel momentarily insignificant.

In a million unique ways—as we change diapers, eat dinner, return e-mails, pay the bills—we are to be the evidence of God. Jesus factored in the mundane. We need to eat and sleep and shower and clean up and work on our marriages because of the way he made us— typical, inadequate, and human. Embrace the common: a Sunday afternoon watching sports, Starbucks with a friend, cooking dinner for a neighbor, taking the dog for a walk, heading to a job that is making you more humble and needy because it is so unfulfilling, or working through conflict with a friend you have offended. This and more is all part of it.

So do your everyday and your ordinary. Godliness is found and formed in those places. No man or woman greatly used by God has escaped them. Great men and women of God have transformed the mundane, turning neighborhoods into mission fields, parenting into launching the next generation of God's voices, legal work into loving those most hurting, waiting tables into serving and loving in such a way that people see our God.

> Do your everyday and your ordinary. Godliness is found and formed in those places.

Jesus says the way we glorify God, the way we step into his story, is by accomplishing the work God gives us to do. Jesus glorified his father on earth by doing that very thing.

We play our part in his story, and the beauty is, it was what we were made for.

I hate pat answers . . . and the thought that Jesus was the answer to all the problems inside me always felt like one. I never would have said that out loud. I did actually believe he was powerful enough to heal what was broken in me, but I did not know how to take that truth and shove it deep inside of me where it snapped in and felt different.

"Jennie, I think most of us live thinking there is a medium. A place where we can live regular lives and serve God too." Jessica spoke to me honestly in my living room as we stayed up late talking about surrender, talking about why it is so hard for all of us to give in and how few people we know who truly live surrendered lives. Just out of college, Jessica is a friend who lives with us off and on; she feels like part of our family. Jessica is also a humanitarian photographer who captures the stories of the least of these all over the world. She loves us, we love her, and she often helps us survive the chaos our *anythings* have brought us.

> Something about Jesus changes everything— shatters what we thought we were going to do with our lives.

I listened to her statement, still wanting to agree with the majority of people. I used to think the same thing. I flashed back to the first time I read Katie's words as she described trying to live a medium life:

"BUT, I loved Jesus."

Something about Jesus changes everything—shatters what we thought we were going to do with our lives.

C. S. Lewis says, "Christianity is a statement which, if false, is of no importance, and if true, of infinite importance. The one thing it cannot be is moderately important."[7] If God is real, there is no medium.

## turning over

Throughout Scripture trusting God was always pretty intense. Actually it required near insanity. Moses raised a stick over the Red Sea; Joshua told everyone to walk around a wall seven times and then scream and blow horns; David picked up stones to kill a giant; the disciples waited on a Spirit to fill them before they did anything. All of it took an almost silly amount of faith in a person—not a religion or an idea. These men were trusting in the person of God. They were leaning into what they knew of his character and what he was leading them to do. But no one around them thought they were sane.

God is still not very practical, and to follow him takes trust. Following him completely requires belief that he is good even if everything here and now is not, that he sees us and has an intentional plan for our few years here. We trust in a spiritual person who leads us to do spiritual things that may not totally make sense.

The best analogy I can think of is the show *The Biggest Loser*, where overweight contestants go to a remote ranch to train, diet, and compete to see who can lose the most weight in seven months. What happens to them in the weeks they live on the ranch is pretty radical. They probably sign a contract when they arrive, pledging their will, choices, and desires over to the trainers. They must say to them, "You can have me for anything while I am here." And then everything begins to transform as they fully trust and obey the trainers. But it is hard.

Following Christ got intense for the disciples. These men were stretched beyond human limits and mocked for seeming to follow something ridiculous. When some of the disciples were leaving Christ because it was getting too hard, too costly, Jesus looked up at his men and asked, "Will you leave me too?" (John 6:67 paraphrased).

Bekah and I sat over sushi, talking about following God and how costly it had been getting lately for both of us. She and her husband, Brandon, were leading a group of neighbors and friends through a study on marriage. Many people came because Brandon and Bekah had pursued and loved them for years.

I asked how ministry was going. She vented in dramatically passionate Bekah fashion, "The hardest part is I just get selfish and lazy . . . the hardest part is this world and all its glitter . . . the hardest part is being pulled by the temporary . . . the hardest part is resisting the work of the devil . . . the hardest part is SIN."

I laughed at her, but I agreed.

When it was getting hard on the disciples, Jesus asked them, "Will you leave me too?" And they all shook their heads and replied, "Lord, to whom shall we go?" (John 6:67–68).

To whom do we go but to Jesus?

We were made for God. To be filled with him, to live out our days for him, and to long for the day we will meet him. The minute Adam and Eve turned from him to their pride, they were lost and restless, searching for the fulfillment that only he could bring them. We've all followed suit . . . searching, longing, waiting, but not running to our Jesus. See, he always had an elaborate yet simple plan to get us back.

To die.

So when he looks back at me and says, *Okay now, Jennie, you die. Die to this life and your will and your need to be important and comfortable and happy*, he has my attention.

As we were about to pay our bill and finish dinner, Bekah leaned forward and said, "I have been a Christian for almost thirty years and yet I would say that over the past couple years, I've just now started to grasp how much he really does love me. I've been so programmed to perform as a 'follower of Christ,' and all God ever wanted was for me to surrender, to set aside the agenda and to follow. How easy, yet how challenging, when the world and even the church told or showed me the 'agenda' of what a Christian should be like, act like, look like. It's so refreshing to live now."

I know we are afraid of anything too radical or costly. I used to think I would find life in the medium. But I just felt more stuck, somewhere in the wardrobe . . . with my heart divided, with a vague sense that both worlds existed. But it was really numb and boring and empty, to be honest. Now that I have tasted being *all in*, I don't want medium. We weren't made for medium.

> Now that I have tasted being *all in*, I don't want medium. We weren't made for medium.

Abandonment only makes sense if there is a God worthy of abandoning everything for. The greatest gift in surrender is that in letting go of everything you think will fix you and make you feel better, you find a person . . .

not a pat answer or a verse or a cause. After your head clears from the struggle of wrestling yourself to the ground, you see a person.

He was there before when you were preoccupied, but now you see him.

Jesus said, "These things I have spoken to you, that my joy may be in you, and that your joy may be full" (John 15:11).

The context and the beauty of this prayer is that we see Jesus speaking to his father. We see into their relationship and their love for each other. Jesus existed to please his father. His father met every need he had for wisdom, direction, purpose, love, relationship, and hope. There is something infectious about the way they interact, the sheer delight that Christ had done all that his father has asked, the joy and love and submission Christ has for his father.

"We love because he first loved us" (1 John 4:19).

When we don't love or feel joy or peace or passion, it's because we do not know his love or his joy or peace or passion. He is a person, not a magic pill you take when your life or your soul is broken. He is a person. He is a person you talk to and listen to and love and respect. He's someone you decide to spend time with and dream with, whom you follow and learn from and hurt with, and to whom you ask things— someone you choose over anybody else, over anything else. He is a person—*the* person who defines my life, sweeps in and changes me. When I let him in.

We all want to be free, joyful, and peaceful, but we get reluctant to hand God everything. But that is part of the path to the things he promises us.

## all in

When I was in high school, I went to the beach with some friends. I had always wanted to bungee jump. That was back when I was stupid. We signed up and paid our money. While I was on the ground reading the brochure, laughing with friends about how cool this was going to be, it all seemed so easy. There was very little cost.

Then they make you walk up by yourself. You leave your friends and the laughter and the safety of the ground, and on the top of the tower, looking over the edge, you realize this is serious. You actually have to jump. I think by law they can't push you. So I had to actually put action to all the words I'd thrown out on the ground. I had to jump and completely trust the harness and the eighteen-year-old dude who put it on me.

> At some point, our faith and our words must become our actions and lives.

At some point, our faith and our words must become our actions and lives.

Do we talk more about God than we obey him? We aren't going to get to heaven and have God say, "Thanks for talking about doing so much for me with your friends. That was awesome!" Many of us have sat in Bible studies or retreats or church talking about what we want to change and how we want to live for God, only to go home and back to the routine of life.

Change is a funny thing. It takes change to change.

But here is the beautiful, backward thing about risking everything for God: it is not the friends on the ground cutting up and checking out the brochure finding life; it is the one on the tower with everything at risk, heart racing, hopes high, purpose clear, and completely dependent and scared to death who is really experiencing life.

It takes risking everything on a God that is invisible. Our God is terribly jealous for us. And when we are on towers, trusting in him alone, he has us.

It's so easy to live on the ground. But in light of what is to come? In light of a God who adores us and who is calling us to eternal and lasting things? In light of these spiritual realities, our caution makes us look ridiculous.

We jump because he jumped. Jesus prayed his guts out for us, our joy, our mission, our future with him . . . and twenty-four hours later he bled out on a cross for us. And there was joy in that for him, all because in pouring out his life he was restoring mankind to himself. In his death there was life.

The road to life, to freedom, is death. "We know that our old self was crucified with him in order that the body of sin might be brought to nothing, so that we would no longer be enslaved to sin" (Rom. 6:6).

The problem with following Jesus is he does things backward—freedom and true life came out of his death. In turn, to follow Christ to the cross, we jump, trusting him with everything, praying *anything*, handing over every day and all that lives in it to a person—in death we find life and freedom too.

I want life. I want the kind of life found on towers with my God, heart-pounding, eternity-changing life.

# better dreams
## poured out

When my oldest son, Conner, was nine, he was really into cars. He knew the names of every Porsche and Lamborghini, and the way he would talk about the $300,000 price tag and wanting to own one made my stomach turn over. It wasn't necessarily that the cars cost so much—I have things that cost too much (not that much), but still that was relative. I just wanted more for him. We aren't meant to be content with metal. Redemption changed the goal: it is no longer to gather, but to give. We will itch inside until we live for more than the gathering.

We are not foolish to stop gathering and open up our lives to give everything. It will be lost whether we try to save it or not. It is wise to hand it over now and to allow Christ to make something of it—and I assure you, he will.

See, when you push it all in, he is actually going to do something with it. He doesn't burn it on an altar, delighting in meaningless sacrifice. Hosea 6:6 says, "For I desire steadfast love and not sacrifice, the knowledge of God rather than burnt offerings."

There are a lot of people he cares about who need parts of our lives. He actually looks around the planet and points, saying, *Over there—give it to them.* When we walk over there and give it to them, we feel God, his heart and power boiling up. What a privilege to walk near to the heart of God. It is impossible to avoid the call in Scripture to take care of the poor, the widow, the orphan.

"Truly, I say to you, as you did it to one of the least of these my brothers, you did it to me" (Matt. 25:40).

"Whoever oppresses a poor man insults his Maker, but he who is generous to the needy honors him" (Prov. 14:31).

We are the extremities of God, the limbs carrying out his will. We are what he designed to administer his love and care. We see it clearly in John 15, as Christ lays out how God and man will work together. He says, "Stay close to me because you are our limbs . . . you are the branches in which we will produce our fruit. And through the fruit that will be dispersed out of you, a simple branch, our name will be made great. Our glory will be displayed to the world" (vv. 1–11, paraphrased).

> What a privilege to walk near to the heart of God.

I used to feel inconvenienced when I was asked to give. Things have changed. Now I don't want to miss participating in things that last forever. I *want* to give the pieces of my life, my gifts and money, to whomever God says. I don't want to get to heaven and see what I could have been a part of but missed because I was numb or selfish or scared.

I give my life to Jesus because I trust him, and freedom and hope are found in him alone. But practically speaking, he's going to do something with my life when I give it to him. He has a plan for it. It is not a meaningless sacrifice.

Jesus takes normal, numb lives and pours them over the lives of those in need. When your excess is poured out over the hurting, those in need of God, of healing, of food or water . . . all of a sudden what you thought mattered doesn't matter anymore.

## extra bedrooms

There is a movement in the church right now that resonates with many of our souls because we were meant for so much more than the American dream. It resonates because, in order to pursue the welfare of others, especially the marginalized, an element of death is involved; it costs something. Financially, yes, but bigger than that, it costs our comfort. The motto of this movement is "Do something."

No doubt, when we teeter on the edge of the tower before leaping away from our comfort, we find more of God. We experience more of his heart and his Spirit. Now I know what my seminary professor meant when he talked about finding God in risk. God is often present right over the edges. Even so, "doing something," even something good, even something *great*, will never be the gospel. In trusting God with everything, a numb life, which may have seemed to be rather boring and unjoyful and unpeaceful, explodes into something beautifully meaningful.

> God is often present right over the edges.

When Conner talked about wanting expensive cars, I wanted him to dream bigger dreams, better dreams—dreams that would mean more than a car that will rust. I wanted him to dream on behalf of boys who wouldn't dare hope for a ten-dollar soccer ball, for people who don't know there is a God who sees them. I want him to have dreams like that for $300,000. It's not legalism; it's not duty . . . it's actually joy.

While my prosperity is a gift, I am the dispenser of my gift. I am the channel through which others will prosper. I can take what I need and even enough for some fun and memories and experiences, but I

anything

have hands, feet, the Internet, plane tickets, resources, the gospel, and money so that God can use me to recklessly save, recklessly heal, recklessly love. Father Kaj Munk put it so clearly:

What, therefore, is our task today? Should I answer "Faith, hope and love?" That sounds beautiful. But I would say—courage. No, even that is not challenging enough to be the whole truth. Our task today is recklessness. For what we Christians lack is not psychology or literature . . . we lack a holy rage—*the recklessness which comes from the knowledge of God and humanity*. The ability to rage when justice lies prostrate on the streets, and when the lie rages across the face of the earth . . . a holy anger about the things that are wrong in the world. To rage against the ravaging of God's earth and the destruction of God's people. To rage when little children must die of hunger, while the tables of the rich are sagging with food. To rage at the senseless killing of so many. To rage against complacency. To restlessly seek that recklessness that will challenge and seek to change human history until it conforms to the norms of the kingdom of God.[8]

We want God to knock out suffering and poverty. Ironically, he gave us just about all we need to do it. We give our lives to him and he gives our lives away. Nothing on earth is more fun and more full than being distributed by an all-knowing, compassionate God who knows exactly where our ridiculously blessed lives would be best spent.

We have been blessed to watch friend after friend pray the prayer of *anything*. God has flooded them with purpose, exposing little cracks in the earth that they were perfectly designed to fill. Some of our friends own a beauty school here. They wanted to be used in some greater way to help women in Rwanda. One of the best ways to empower the women is to give them a way to financially provide for their families. Our friends are about to open Africa New Life Beauty School. Women for years to come will be trained in a trade and be able to provide a future for their families. And our friends feel that was easy—it just flowed out of the resources they already possessed. There are a million creative ways to give our lives away. God is just waiting.

At the end of the day, we live in a generation that cannot ignore what we know about the poor. We know more than any other generation; we see it on TV and the Internet—it's all over. The reality is that while we have two cars, extra bedrooms, and constantly worry about eating too much, downtrodden people are dying on streets alone. What a privilege to be in positions to do something about it for at least one.

> Nothing on earth is more fun and more full than being distributed by an all-knowing, compassionate God who knows exactly where our ridiculously blessed lives would be best spent.

Wherever you are, there are people in need both spiritually and physically. Where does God want to take your plenty and pour it out? The vision that God woke me up with the night of my birthday came because there are many people who are starving spiritually. Through seminary and great churches and mentors and study, he had given me a lot of spiritual food to pass out to those starving people. And many of you reading this are the same. You have done dozens of Bible studies or been in church your entire life and you have a lot to give away. But God doesn't let us just feed people spiritually—he clearly calls us to take our plenty and give it to care for people in physical need too. Christ sacrificially and deeply cared for the physical and spiritual needs of people. May it be said of us, our generation, the same.

We love because he first loved us.

We die because he first died.

We give because he gave everything.

My car-loving son Conner is now eleven. He was beside me when I met those four joyful, passionate men in Rwanda. He was beside me with arms raised worshipping with boys his age who came off the streets for a warm meal but first closed their eyes and lifted their hands and with all their heart thanking their Jesus. My son was with me when we met his brother for the first time in a gloomy orphanage with a hundred other little children who wouldn't be getting in cars that day with a new mom and dad.

**Where does God want to take your plenty and pour it out?**

After we got home, I went for a walk with Conner. Early on, he was the slowest to get on board with the idea of adoption. I remembered him tearing up when I sensed his reluctance, and he said, "Mom, I want to help orphans and all, but this is really going to be a lot for me." He was the one headed into teen years and looking at sharing his room with a toddler, and he was not as eager about change in general. He was losing control of his life and losing the special place of being the only son all at the same time.

But on this day, after we got home from Africa, I asked him how he was doing. He shook his head. "Mom, I never knew how blessed I was. I just see now that I have so much for a reason. I want God to use me. I am responsible for all I have been given—responsible for using it for those who have not been given all of this."

He's dreaming bigger dreams . . . dreaming better dreams.

# wind

everything different

I closed my eyes. It was almost painfully loud. I could hear my four kids screaming at the top of their lungs as my husband roared through the house chasing them. If he caught any one of them they were going to be ruthlessly tickled. They knew it, so they ran pretty fast, screaming. Cooper was running by far the fastest, his legs already straight and strong, no longer in need of braces. I was about to head out the door to finish the last few chapters of this book. But I closed my eyes for a minute to take in the chaos of a new life—the consequences of a simple prayer.

In two years, everything was different. Our family had grown with the light of a dark-skinned, busy, passionate boy. I had thought we were laying down our lives for him, and instead he breathed life and joy into us. He's a boy who captures the heart of every person he meets. He rushed in intensely carrying joy and fervor and unloaded it on our family. Now his position in our family was declaring the gospel louder than any other thing I've experienced.

I had a job—a pretty demanding one where I poured out words almost daily, telling about my Jesus. My days were spent torn between training a new toddler in how to speak English and use a fork, and meeting deadlines and trying to explain invisible, important things in writing. I knew I could never really do justice to either. But peace came in because I knew I was doing the things God put me here for just a little while to do. I was living the story that he had written for me—eyes laser focused on one: the God who had called me. It was full and right, even though a lot of days I fight inadequacy and fear. I never would have dreamed any of this two years ago.

> The winds had changed in our lives. We completely vacated the cruise ship and found ourselves on some nimble Navy battleship. We were on a mission.

Our church had changed. As Zac prayed about his future and the church he had poured into and dreamed of for years, God began leading him and the elders to consider partnering with another gospel-centered, missional church to more fully reach the city. Six years ago God gave my husband a vision to lead a church full of missionaries, and now they could see that vision was going to be best realized by joining another church in town that was changing the world because it had the hand of God on it. Our church was healthy and strong and people were growing, and yet these men sensed God's calling to unite and give up control for the sake of the gospel. Zac let go of directional leadership of the church. It was a little death for the sake of forever, because he trusted that God was real and worth following even into uncharted territory.

Our priorities changed too. We were praying about moving to a less expensive house and doing things like canceling cable so we could spend less, because Zac wanted to keep taking our kids back to Africa, and I wanted to sponsor every child I could rather than have our lives be perfectly comfortable.

My days, Zac's days, my family, and Christmas cards changed forever, all because of a prayer. But even with all that, all the craziness and chaos, that is not what felt most different. The winds had changed in our lives. We completely vacated the cruise ship and found ourselves on some nimble navy battleship. We were on a mission. We were inspired. We were full and passionate and joyful. We were running with all our might with barely a second to think too much about it or analyze it. God's Spirit unleashed himself around us, and we were doing our best to just keep up and hang on. We had seen more of God in two years than we had in our entire lives.

I originally thought we were going to have to be such martyrs, to suffer for Christ and pour out our lives unto death. I was wrong. He was desperately pouring himself into us, his joy and passion, sustaining us each day with peace that he was real and we were exactly where he wanted us. God had wanted our hearts, not any dramatic sacrifice. These weren't radical sacrifices, just simple obedience. We were just following an all-knowing God whom we completely trusted. And it was all turning out to be fun and full of life and joy.

> God had wanted our hearts, not any dramatic sacrifice.

This was life. This was what Jesus meant when he said, "You will receive power when the Holy Spirit has come upon you, and you will be my witnesses in Jerusalem and in all Judea and Samaria, and to the end of the earth" (Acts 1:8).

You are going to change the world with my Spirit and for my fame on this earth. And this helper will "teach you all things and bring to your remembrance all that I have said to you" (John 14:26).

This is something totally different, backward, but this mission is clear; it is what we are designed for.

Jesus was the fulfillment of the story. Through him we see God, and through faith in his death and resurrection we are set apart for eternity with him. *But* it is through his Spirit that we are able to do what he wants us to do here.

Zac says the reason we don't see much of the Holy Spirit in the church today is that we are not abandoned to his mission. The Spirit was given to us for *a purpose*: to make him known here and in the heavens where the angels watch as the cosmic war between good and evil, God and the devil plays out through us. It's insane . . . I know.

Jesus knew they could not live this life without the Spirit inside them. So at Pentecost, after Jesus had left, a wind blew and the Spirit came. He filled them, he poured out himself into them. And these men with previously common and mundane lives started to preach with no fear, heal the suffering, and start churches that would go on to carry the gospel all the way to us two thousand years later. They were average men full of the Spirit, abandoned, committed to the mission of God.

A good friend of mine went to visit Katie in Uganda. When she got back I asked her to tell me everything, sure that Katie would have left an afterglow on anyone she would ever meet. Instead, my friend said, "Jennie, she's just a regular girl. You'd love her, but she's just a normal girl." She is just a normal girl filled with an extraordinary God who is using her for extraordinary purposes, all because she said yes.

> God's Spirit is essential. Otherwise words like *anything* fall to the ground, meaning nothing, changing nothing.

God's Spirit is essential. Otherwise words like *anything* fall to the ground, meaning nothing, changing nothing.

wind

## the beginning

I closed my eyes. This time a different kind of chaos swirled around me. I listened as a dear friend tried to breathe. Her husband had walked out a few hours before, leaving her with three young kids. He said he never really loved God or her. Everything was spinning.

*Anything* hadn't cost me much yet, really.

It took me back to the conversations with my friend Karen whose husband had died, who felt too afraid that God may take something else as costly if she gave it all to him. It took me back to the orphanage full of children who were not getting in cars with mothers and fathers that day.

God hates divorce and suffering, and he hates death. These are the enemies; these aren't God's desires. The story is just not over yet. All the battles aren't fought and tied up with pretty little bows. God is still blowing through this world on a mission, securing his people, establishing his kingdom, reconciling the hurt and the damage the enemy has caused.

I tremble as I write this, but if he allows one of my children or my husband to die, or if I get cancer, or if we lose all we own to bankruptcy, will I take this back? Will I wish I'd never said God could have me for anything?

> The story is just not over yet. All the battles aren't fought and tied up with pretty little bows.

I've watched as Matt Chandler, a well-known pastor in Dallas, has shared his walk through his battle with brain cancer.[9] He is a man living surrendered. He was surrendered before cancer. And we've all watched, through his sermons and his updates, how he's kept a glimmer in his eye, as though he knows a good secret. It's as though he knows about the other side, and no matter what happens, it is going to be okay. He knows that even if the worst happened here, it would only last a few minutes compared to forever. He didn't just preach about heaven; he held on to it as his home, as his hope, as the glimmer in his eye facing death.

There's more than this.

"Father, I desire that they also, whom you have given me, may be with me where I am, to see my glory that you have given me because you loved me before the foundation of the world" (John 17:24).

The next day after those words, Jesus would go die the most brutal death possible. But that paled in light of the glimmer he held in his eye that night he talked to his father.

As if he were letting us in on the secret, Jesus whispered back to his father, *This will all be worth it. Wait till they are with us and see our glory. Just wait till all of this work and suffering and pouring out is over and we are in heaven together forever. Just wait.*

A day is coming when our eyes will close and there will be no more chaos. No one will be preaching or writing books about God to help us remember, because we will be alive in that world with him forever.

*Anything* is nothing in light of that.
In light of forever. In light of him.

# what is your anything?

I believe that like every generation before us, we have an opportunity to see God move in our midst . . . to surrender in such a way that we would turn the head and heart of God. He waits for surrendered lives, and he finds them, he floods them; I want to be a part of that.

If my people who are called by my name humble themselves, and pray and seek my face and turn from their wicked ways, then I will hear from heaven and will forgive their sin and heal their land. (2 Chron. 7:14)

Praying *anything* is not saying mere words or reckless sacrifice; praying *anything* begins with love—actually loving a person. "If I give away all I have, and if I deliver up my body to be burned, but have not love, I gain nothing" (1 Cor. 13:3).

## experience Christ

*Anything* begins with a relationship with the God of the universe through Christ. He says, "I am the way, and the truth, and the life. No one comes to the Father except through me" (John 14:6).

Pressing down all we love more than him is next, and that may take a while. It took thirty years of God chipping away at me until the bathroom floor eperience, and even still it is a daily surrender.

But after that—after you are all surrendered, willing, abandoned, sold out, and all in—then what?

## pray

Our story began long before we prayed. The night we uttered the words was just a step in the process of surrender. But it was an important step. God wants to be invited in to lead our lives, for your heart to truly stand before God and say, "You have me. Do anything with me." That is a bold, beautiful move. Continuing to mean it daily as his will unfolds will prove even more powerful. Ask him to show you where he wants you to pour out your life and gifts and resources.

## God speaks

God speaks first through his Word. If I hadn't read God's Word to us about caring for the poor and the orphan dozens of times, I would have never heard his Spirit leading me to adopt. Or if it wasn't clear to me the passionate way Christ loved me and poured his life out for me, I would not be compelled to do the same for others. We know who God is because of his Word; we must read it. His Spirit's leading always is tied up in his Word. We are to walk with God "in spirit and truth" (John 4:24). One without the other is not of God; it is either a false spirit or dead religion.

So you read and study and search and pray. Then you ask God to lead you. When we were feeling led in certain specific *anythings*, it wasn't through an audible voice. It was through promptings in our spirits, a burning in your gut when you know something is real. It burns, but it is also subtle and gently, mysteriously quiet. Sometimes it makes itself clear quickly and sometimes it involves months of processing and wrestling with God till we know for sure. But he does still speak because he has things for us here—things we cannot accomplish unless we hear from him.

## band together

Surround yourself with people on the same mission. We were built to need people. We cannot passionately surrender and follow God alone. We were built for bands of brothers (or sisters) to fight beside us. Find a church, start a study or small group, get creative, but find people to live on a mission with who will make you better, help you remember, and help you live your *anythings*. Intentionally pursue people who make you better.

## obey

Do what he says—whatever he says. Like Jonah running from the Ninevites in the Bible, you will be miserable running, miserable until you obey. Even if it is hard, even it is costly, it will be worth it. No matter the cost . . . obey and trust him with the consequences of that obedience. He is worth it. He is worth forsaking everything. We've boiled him down to principles. Yet, everything else I have ever tried to smash into my soul to fill it seems to just make me ache for more. He gets in and actually restores me, unwinds my mess of a head and soul. His mercy trumps the most epic of stories. This God is real and he is worth my surrender.

# acknowledgments

I would have never saved myself. I am too selfish and too prideful. I would have kept on pretending I knew God—unless in his mercy, he stepped in on a hot night by a campfire and saved me. You blew in God—you blew into my soul in front of crosses; you blew into my bathroom that night on my floor; you blew in to lead us in our *anythings* and give us strength to follow you; you blew in to give me words to make you known. How ridiculous it would be to ever take an inch of credit.

God, for you and because of you these words exist. Take all glory and may your name expand through a simple girl and some black-and-white words on pages.

I would have never known God unless someone had told me about him. Thank you Mom and Dad for not just telling me about him but showing him to me as you lived sacrificially raising me. You do not worship a plastic god. He is real to you and he pours out on everyone who knows you.

## acknowledgments

I would never have prayed *anything* without someone holding my hand and whispering the words first. Thank you, Zac, for leading me and loving me and pushing me to these uncomfortable places of making God known. I never meant to write, and you pushed me to do so. May God reward you greatly for your humility and courage in allowing me to be used by God.

I would have never published a book without someone believing in me and seeing God's hand on my life. Jessica Taylor, you built things beside me over many sleepless nights when we would not have dared dream they would go out to the world. Steve Laube, you saw something across a table with your Simon Cowell cynicism. You first believed in me by becoming my agent. And Debbie Wickwire, sitting over chips and enchiladas saw something in me, and since then you have bled and cried and lost sleep beside me. God in his mercy gave me an editor who is a friend, a mentor, and without you, this book would not exist.

Nothing would exist without teams of people to set this in motion. Thank you, Thomas Nelson. The first time I came to Nelson, they swiftly ushered me into a room full of people—there must have been twenty or more. I was so nervous. The meeting was epic, a moment when life changes and you ponder for months following, almost positive it was only a dream. That day each team member looked at me and said, "We want to build the things you are dreaming about Jennie, all of them." Days like that feel like dreams because they almost always are.

That day in the conference room when you all promised moons and threw in stars . . . every day since you have delivered moons and stars. I pray God moves mightily through all of our work together.

# notes

## Part 1: Everything Keeping Us from Anything

1. A. W. Tozer, *The Knowledge of the Holy* (New York: HarperOne, 1978), 1.
2. "How Deep the Father's Love for Us," Stuart Townsend.
3. Charles Swindoll, *The Grace Awakening* (Nashville: Thomas Nelson, 2003), 79-80.
4. Oswald Chambers, http://www.brainyquote.com/quotes/authors/o/oswald_chambers.html
5. Tim Keller, "Counterfeit Gods" (speech given at the 2010 Gospel Coalition Conference, March 7, 2010), http://thegospelcoalition.org/resources/a/counterfeit_gods.
6. Ibid.
7. Sermon and resources available at www.thedevilisreal.com.
8. Rick Riordan, *The Lightning Thief* (New York: Hyperion Books, 2011), paraphrased.

## Part 2: Praying Anything

1. Katie Davis, "Well Since You Asked," Kisses from Katie (blog), April 2, 2009, http://kissesfromkatie.blogspot.com/2009/04/well-since-you-asked.html.
2. Davis, www.kissesfromkatie.blogspot.com.

3. Todd Harper, "Our Contract with God: An Interview with Bill and Vonette Bright," http://library.generousgiving.org/articles/display.asp?id=123.

4. Jennie Allen, "Revival," Wrestling with the Invisible (blog), April 20, 2009, http://jennieallen.com/uncategorized/revival/.

5. Paul Dwight Moody and Arthur Percy Fitt, *The Shorter Life of D. L. Moody* (1900: repr., Charleston: Nabu Press, 2010). 41.

6. William Revell Moody, *The Life of Dwight L. Moody* (1900; repr., Charleston: Forgotten Books, 2010, 134).

7. Jim Elliot, *The Journals of Jim Elliot*, ed. Elisabeth Elliot (1978; repr., Grand Rapids: Revell, 2002, 174).

8. A. W. Tozer, *The Pursuit of God* (1957; repr., Camp Hill, PA: WingSpread, 2007 ), 97.

9. Jennie Allen, "Falling into Grace," Wrestling with the Invisible (blog) September 28, 2010, http://jennieallen.com/writing/falling-into-obedience/.

10. Oswald Chambers, *My Utmost for His Highest: An Updated Edition in Today's Language* (Grand Rapids: Discovery House, 1992), 16, emphasis added.

11. Ibid., 17, emphasis added.

## Part 3: Living Anything

1. John Piper, "The Centrality of the Glory of God," desiringGod (blog), November 4, 2009, http://www.desiringgod.org/blog/posts/the-centrality-of-the-glory-of-god.

2. Tyler Merrick, (Tweet), July 8, 2011, http://twitter.com/#!/tylermerrick/status/78576598093271040.

3. Henri J. M. Nouwen, *Reaching Out* (New York: Doubleday, 1986), 16.

4. Jennie Allen, "Curtains and Cute Lives," Wrestling with the Invisible (blog), August 6, 2009, http://jennieallen.com/uncategorized/curtains-and-cute-lives/.

5. Jennie Allen, "Behind the Scenes of My Life," Wrestling with the Invisible (blog), April 15, 2010, http://jennieallen.com/uncategorized/behind-the-scenes-of-my-life/.

6. Philip Gourevitch, *We Wish to Inform You That Tomorrow We Will Be Killed with Our Families* (New York: Picador, 1999).

7. C. S. Lewis, *God in the Dock* (Grand Rapids: Eerdmans, 1994), 101.

8. Kaj Munk, as quoted by Shane Claiborne in *The Irresistible Revolution* (Grand Rapids: Zondervan, 2006), 294, emphasis added.

9. Matt's blog entries can be found at http://fm.thevillagechurch.net/blog/pastors/. See also http://mobile.twitter.com//MattChandler74.

# about the author

Jennie Allen's passion is to communicate a bigger God through writing and teaching. She graduated from Dallas Theological Seminary with a master's in Biblical studies and is blessed to serve alongside her husband, Zac, in ministry. They have four children, including their youngest son who was recently adopted from Rwanda.